MARILYN HICKEY

TIME
with
HIM

365 days

of refreshing, peace,
and hope in His presence

Time with Him
365 Days of Refreshing, Peace, and Hope in His Presence

Copyright © 2018
Marilyn Hickey

Marilyn Hickey Ministries
P.O. Box 6598
Englewood, Colorado 80155-6598

All Rights Reserved

Printed in the United States of America
ISBN 978-0-9963685-9-9

Unless otherwise indicated, all Scripture quotations are taken from the Holy Bible, the New International Version . Copyright © 1973, 1978, 1984, 2011 by Biblica, Inc. ™Used by permission of Zondervan. All rights reserved worldwide. www.zondervan.com The "NIV" and "New International Version" are trademarks registered in the United States Patent and Trademark Office by Biblica, Inc.™

Scripture quotations marked (NKJV) are taken from the Holy Bible, New King James Version©. Copyright©1982 by Thomas Nelson. Used by permission. All rights reserved.

Scripture quotations marked (ISV) are taken from the Holy Bible, International Standard Version©. Copyright©1982 by Thomas Nelson. Used by permission. All rights reserved.

Scripture quotations marked (ESV) are taken from the Holy Bible, English Standard Version©. Copyright©1982 by Thomas Nelson. Used by permission. All rights reserved.

Scripture quotations marked (MEV) are taken from the Modern English Version. Copyright © 2014 by Military Bible Association. Used by permission. All rights reserved.

Scripture quotations marked (MSG) are taken from The Message. Copyright © 1993, 1994, 1995, 1996, 2000, 2001, 2002. Used by permission of NavPress Publishing Group.

Scripture quotations marked (NLT) are taken from the Holy Bible, New Living Translation, copyright © 1996, 2004, 2007, 2013, 2015 by Tyndale House Foundation. Used by permission of Tyndale House Publishers, Inc., Carol Stream, Illinois 60188. All rights reserved.

www.marilynandsarah.org

JANUARY 1
Genesis 1, 2; Matthew 1

Our thought for today is **IMAGE OF GOD.**

So God created man in His own image: in the image of God He created him; male and female He created them (Genesis 1:27, NKJV).

Everyone is made so uniquely, yet we are all made in the image of God. This means that we can find our identity in Christ—all things are possible when we walk in our righteous identity through Christ.

PRAY FOR: AFGHANISTAN

JANUARY 2
Genesis 3, 4; Matthew 2

Our word for today is **SHEPHERD.**

"But you, Bethlehem... out of you will come a Ruler Who will shepherd My people Israel" (Matthew 2:6, NKJV).

Jesus is our shepherd. When we know His voice, we are led by Him and can trust that He watches over us. He is nurturing and healing His flock—He deeply cares for you!

PRAY FOR: ALBANIA

JANUARY 3
Genesis 5, 6, 7; Matthew 3, 4

Our thought for today is **MY COVENANT**.

"But I will establish My covenant with you; and you shall go into the ark..." (Genesis 6:18, NKJV).

When God established His covenant with Noah, He protected Noah and his family in the ark and provided for their needs. When Jesus established His covenant with us, He kept it for us because we couldn't—He continues to provide for us because of His covenant. He is our provider!

PRAY FOR: ALGERIA

JANUARY 4
Genesis 8, 9; Matthew 5

Our thought for today is **MY RAINBOW**.

"I set My rainbow in the cloud, and it shall be for the sign of the covenant between Me and the earth" (Genesis 9:13, NKJV).

When God placed the rainbow in the sky, He intended it as a reminder of His promise that the earth would never again be destroyed by a flood. Likewise, when we see the Cross, we are reminded that Jesus has redeemed us from eternal destruction.

PRAY FOR: AMERICAN SAMOA

JANUARY 5
Genesis 10, 11; Matthew 6

Our word for today is **FORGIVE**.

*"But if you do not **forgive** men their sins, your Father will not forgive your sins"* (Matthew 6:15).

Unforgiveness puts roots in us that go deep. These roots can produce some really bad things when we allow them to take over. God says that we should forgive others; when we forgive, it can produce great fruit in our lives!

PRAY FOR: ANDORRA

JANUARY 6
Genesis 12, 13; Matthew 7

Our word for today is **BLESS**.

*"I will bless those who **bless** you, and whoever curses you I will curse; and all peoples on earth will be blessed through you"* (Genesis 12:3).

God loves His people. He heals us, restores us and blesses us! And just as we are blessed by the Father, we are called to bless others. This verse says that all the people on earth will be blessed through Believers, those who have been grafted into the family of Abraham! Extend the blessings you have received to those around you.

PRAY FOR: ANGOLA

JANUARY 7
Genesis 14, 15; Matthew 8

Our thought for today is **A TENTH.**

*King Melchizedek... was serving as the priest of God Most High. Melchizedek blessed Abram... Then Abram gave him **a tenth** of everything* (Genesis 14:18-20, ISV).

God's principle of sowing and reaping releases blessing in our lives. Just as Abram gave a tenth of everything, when we give of our finances, time, or ourselves, the blessings of heaven are poured upon us!

PRAY FOR: ANGUILLA

JANUARY 8
Genesis 16, 17; Matthew 9

Our word for today is **FAITH.**

*Then He touched their eyes, saying, "According to your **faith** let it be to you"* (Matthew 9:29, NKJV).

Even faith as small as a mustard seed can move mountains! Faith in God pleases Him. Even the smallest amount of faith can produce big things.

PRAY FOR: ANTARCTICA

JANUARY 9
Genesis 18, 19; Matthew 10

Our thought for today is **FOR THE LORD.**

"... Why did Sarah laugh... Is anything too hard for the LORD?..." (Genesis 18:13-14, NKJV)

Nothing is too big, too hard, or too challenging for the Lord: Sarah supernaturally conceived and gave birth; the Israelites received manna daily while wandering in the desert; the walls of Jericho fell—these miracles, that seemed impossible to man, were possible for the Lord!

PRAY FOR: ANTIQUA AND BARBUDA

JANUARY 10
Genesis 20, 21, 22; Matthew 11, 12

Our word for today is **REST.**

"Come to Me, all you who labor and are heavy laden, and I will give you rest... For My yoke is easy and My burden is light" (Matthew 11:28, 30, NKJV).

Man's first full day on earth was a day of resting with God. Our rest with God helps us to do the work God calls us to do. When we rest with God first, we can trust that He is helping and guiding us in our work.

PRAY FOR: ARGENTINA

JANUARY 11
Genesis 23, 24; Matthew 13

Our thought for today is **THINGS HIDDEN**.

*"... I will utter **things hidden** since the creation of the world"* (Matthew 13:35).

When we have an open heart and mind to receive God's Word and wisdom, He reveals "things hidden" to us. Pursuing a relationship with the Lord that is rich in conversation is so important to gaining heavenly wisdom.

PRAY FOR: ARMENIA

JANUARY 12
Genesis 25, 26; Matthew 14

Our word for today is **FLOURISH**.

"... Now the LORD has given us room and we will flourish in the land" (Genesis 26:22).

God wants good things for His children. He may lead you into seemingly barren lands, but He will empower you to flourish! Trust Him and His provision for your life.

PRAY FOR: ARUBA

JANUARY 13
Genesis 27, 28; Matthew 15

Our word for today is **COMPASSION.**

Jesus called his disciples to him and said, "I have compassion for these people..." (Matthew 15:32).

Jesus reminds His disciples of the importance of love and compassion. The Lord has a heart for the suffering of people, and we should, too. We are not called to judge others based on their actions or circumstances, but we are always called to extend love and compassion.

PRAY FOR: AUSTRALIA

JANUARY 14
Genesis 29, 30; Matthew 16

Our thought for today is **SON OF MAN.**

"For the Son of Man is going to come in his Father's glory with his angels..." (Matthew 16:27).

Jesus is not just the Son of God, but He is the Son of Man. One day He will return to earth covered in the Father's glory, for as the Son of Man, a man with flesh and blood, He became a living sacrifice for the sins of the world.

PRAY FOR: AUSTRIA

JANUARY 15
Genesis 31, 32; Matthew 17

Our thought for today is **I WILL BE WITH YOU.**

"*... Return to the land of your fathers and to your family, and I will be with you*" (Genesis 31:3, NKJV).

God's promises never fail! When He says that He will be with us, we can trust His Word. God is with you in both the good and the bad times—through all circumstances, know that God is with you. He will take care of you in your circumstances!

PRAY FOR: AZERBAIJAN

JANUARY 16
Genesis 33, 34; Matthew 18

Our word for today is **HUMBLE.**

"*... whoever **humbles** himself as this little child is the greatest in the kingdom of heaven*" (Matthew 18:4, NKJV).

Throughout Scripture, we are told of the importance of being like a child. As a child of God, we can keep this is mind as we practice humility and grace in our daily lives.

PRAY FOR: BAHAMAS

JANUARY 17
Genesis 35, 36, 37; Matthew 19, 20

Our word for today is **POSSIBLE**.

*Jesus looked at them and said, "With man this is impossible, but with God all things are **possible**"* (Matthew 19:26).

No situation is impossible for God. He can and will interrupt the devil's plans and change a curse into a blessing. He makes everything possible!

PRAY FOR: BAHRAIN

JANUARY 18
Genesis 38, 39; Matthew 21

Our word for today is **SUCCESS**.

*"...the LORD was with him and...gave him **success** in everything he did."* (Genesis 39:3).

When you walk with the Lord and are aware of His presence in your life, you will see how He brings success to your endeavors. He wants the best for you as His child and will delight in helping you succeed!

PRAY FOR: BANGLADESH

JANUARY 19
Genesis 40, 41; Matthew 22

Our word for today is **LOVE**.

"...Love the LORD *your God with all your heart, with all your soul, and with all your mind"* (Matthew 22:37, NKJV).

What seems like such a simple command can often be so difficult for people. Loving God with your heart, soul and mind is reflected in your actions, words and thoughts. Are you loving God with every part of yourself?

PRAY FOR: BARBADOS

JANUARY 20
Genesis 42, 43; Matthew 23

Our thought for today is **DON'T BE AFRAID**.

*"**Don't be afraid**. Your God, the God of your father, has given you treasure..."* (Genesis 43:23).

We have no reason to fear because our Father is our heavenly protection and power. He gives you authority to rule over darkness, and He shields you from anything that may come against you.

PRAY FOR: BELARUS

JANUARY 21
Genesis 44, 45; Matthew 24

Our word for today is **DELIVERANCE.**

*"But God sent me ahead of you to preserve... and to save your lives by a great **deliverance**"* (Genesis 45:7).

No situation is too challenging or difficult for the God Who loves you. Call upon Him today in your need and He will be faithful to deliver you from your troubles.

PRAY FOR: BELGIUM

JANUARY 22
Genesis 46, 47; Matthew 25

Our word for today is **MASTER.**

*"... Well done, good and faithful servant!... Come and share your **master's** happiness!"* (Matthew 25:23).

As believers, we can serve God through our actions, our relationships, our worship, and so many other areas. God is our loving Father and our righteous Master, deserving of our praise.

PRAY FOR: BELIZE

JANUARY 23
Genesis 48, 49; Matthew 26

Our word for today is **INCREASE.**

"...I am going to make you fruitful and will increase your numbers..." (Genesis 48:4).

The storehouses of heaven have a limitless supply! God wants to increase every area of your life. While it's easy to think of increase as financial, He also wants to increase your JOY—HOPE—PEACE every day.

PRAY FOR: BENIN

JANUARY 24
Genesis 50; Exodus 1, 2; Matthew 27, 28

Our word for today is **GOOD.**

*"You intended to harm me, but God intended it for **good** to accomplish what is now being done..."* (Genesis 50:20).

God is not just good, He is very, very good! All His actions toward us are good, all the fruit produced in our life through Him is good and every thought He has about you is good. He is a good, good God!

PRAY FOR: BERMUDA

JANUARY 25
Exodus 3, 4; Mark 1

Our thought for today is **KINGDOM OF GOD.**

*"... The **kingdom of God** is near. Repent and believe the good news!"* (Mark 1:15)

We are citizens of a kingdom that is eternal. Our King and Lord will never pass away. He will always rule justly and is known for extending outrageous acts of mercy. We are so blessed to be a part of His kingdom while living here on earth!

PRAY FOR: BHUTAN

JANUARY 26
Exodus 5, 6; Mark 2

Our word for today is **SABBATH.**

*Then he said to them, "The **Sabbath** was made for man, not man for the Sabbath"* (Mark 2:27).

A day of rest—the love of God is so deep and abiding that He declared a whole day for man to rest and enjoy the peace of His presence. Take time this week to participate in the Sabbath that He provided.

PRAY FOR: BOLIVIA

JANUARY 27
Exodus 7, 8; Mark 3

Our thought for today is **LORD OUR GOD.**

"... It will be as you say, so that you may know there is no one like the LORD our God" (Exodus 8:10).

It is amazing that because of the work of Christ on the cross, you can experience intimacy with the One Who is the Lord our God. The Creator of all things desires intimate relationship with you today. He is never too big to abide with you and He is never too small to defeat your problems.

PRAY FOR: BOSNIA AND HERZEGOVINA

JANUARY 28
Exodus 9, 10; Mark 4

Our word for today is **PROCLAIMED.**

"... I have raised you up ... that my name might be proclaimed in all the earth" (Exodus 9:16).

The power that comes from speaking out what God has done in your life is a wonderful thing! Proclaim today all that He has done and is doing for you. His love never changes and you are His witness on this earth.

PRAY FOR: BOTSWANA

JANUARY 29
Exodus 11, 12; Mark 5

Our thought for today is **GO IN PEACE.**

He said to her, "Daughter, your faith has healed you. Go in peace and be freed from your suffering" (Mark 5:34).

Jesus is the "Jehovah-Shalom" in the Bible, which tells us that Jesus is our peace. Part of redemption is having the presence and peace of the Lord, which enables us to walk peacefully in our daily lives.

PRAY FOR: BRAZIL

JANUARY 30
Exodus 13, 14; Mark 6

Our thought for today is **TAKE COURAGE.**

... he spoke to them and said, "Take courage! It is I. Don't be afraid." (Mark 6:50).

Trust God to fight your battles. Ignoring popular opinion and trusting God to fight for you requires great courage. He will always provide for His children—trust that promise today.

PRAY FOR: BRUNEI DARUSSALAM

JANUARY 31
Exodus 15, 16, 17; Mark 7, 8

Our word for today is **STRENGTH.**

*"The LORD is my **strength** and my defense; he has become my salvation..."* (Exodus 15:2).

You're going to have to get into God and let God get into you. We can't falter! We have strength in Christ, and we need it because we have to be strong Christians. More than ever, we need to stand up in prayer for the world and lean on God's strength.

PRAY FOR: BULGARIA

FEBRUARY 1
Exodus 18, 19; Mark 9

Our thought for today is **LITTLE CHILDREN.**

*"Whoever welcomes one of these **little children** in my name welcomes me; and... the one who sent me"* (Mark 9:37).

Are there children in your life today? Maybe not yours, but grandchildren, nieces, nephews? Say a prayer for them; hold them up for a special blessing because Jesus loves the little children.

PRAY FOR: BURKINA FASO

FEBRUARY 2
Exodus 20, 21; Mark 10

Our word for today is **POSSIBLE**.

*Jesus looked at them and said, "With man this is impossible, but not with God; all things are **possible** with God"* (Mark 10:27).

Are you facing a situation that someone has told you will be impossible to defeat? Maybe it's time to stop listening to people and, instead, start listening to the God who makes all things possible.

PRAY FOR: BURUNDI

FEBRUARY 3
Exodus 22, 23; Mark 11

Our word for today is **PREPARED**.

*"...I am sending an angel ahead of you...to bring you to the place I have **prepared**"* (Exodus 23:20).

God prepares the way for you. While we all need a miracle now and then, God has made provision for us to live a lifestyle that is not dependent upon repeated miracles, but is rich in supernatural blessings.

PRAY FOR: CAMBODIA

FEBRUARY 4
Exodus 24, 25; Mark 12

Our thought for today is **LOVE THE LORD.**

"Love the LORD your God with all your heart and with all your soul and with all your mind and with all your strength" (Mark 12:30).

Keeping full of the Word and speaking the Word keeps you full of love. That's where you must be established—in love. When you love the Lord, that love pours out into other areas of your life, too.

PRAY FOR: CAMEROON

FEBRUARY 5
Exodus 26, 27; Mark 13

Our thought for today is **HOLY SPIRIT.**

"... do not worry beforehand about what to say... for it is not you speaking, but the Holy Spirit" (Mark 13:11).

Our flesh will fail. We will say the wrong things and take the wrong actions. But we have the power of the Holy Spirit who will take control for us. Trust that the Holy Spirit will guide your words and actions.

PRAY FOR: CANADA

FEBRUARY 6
Exodus 28, 29; Mark 14

Our word for today is **ANOINT**.

"... anoint and ordain them. Consecrate them so they may serve me as priests" (Exodus 28:41).

I believe the anointing of God can break any curse! Physical, mental, emotional, spiritual... it doesn't matter. We must not accept curses in our lives, but rather accept the anointing of God and know that it is more powerful than anything that may come against us.

PRAY FOR: CAPE VERDE

FEBRUARY 7
Exodus 30, 31, 32; Mark 15, 16

Our word for today is **BOLDLY**.

*Joseph of Arimathea... who was... waiting for the kingdom of God, went **boldly** to Pilate and asked for Jesus' body* (Mark 15:43).

You can break any stronghold that the enemy has on you simply by boldly going after the promises God has made to you. Mark your territory today and know that you can boldly go after what you have been promised!

PRAY FOR: CAYMAN ISLANDS

FEBRUARY 8
Exodus 33, 34; Luke 1

Our thought for today is **MY PRESENCE.**

The LORD replied, "My Presence will go with you, and I will give you rest" (Exodus 33:14).

There is nothing like the presence of God. When we familiarize ourselves with God's presence, we are more aware of it in our lives—it is something that is always with us! His presence is such a blessing.

PRAY FOR: CENTRAL AFRICAN REPUBLIC

FEBRUARY 9
Exodus 35, 36; Luke 2

Our thought for today is **MORE THAN ENOUGH.**

"... The people are bringing more than enough for doing the work the LORD commanded..." (Exodus 36:5).

I've been sowing and tithing for years and I see the rewards of the harvest. It's so good. God doesn't just provide when we do His work, but He provides us with more than enough!

PRAY FOR: CHAD

FEBRUARY 10
Exodus 37, 38; Luke 3

Our word for today is **FIRE**.

"... But one who is more powerful than I will come... He will baptize you with the Holy Spirit and fire'" (Luke 3:16).

Just as you are physically flooded by water in the act of water baptism, so God wants to flood your life with His Own character through the baptism of the Holy Spirit. His character is powerful and dynamic, like fire in your soul.

PRAY FOR: CHILE

FEBRUARY 11
Exodus 39, 40; Luke 4

Our thought for today is **HOLY TO THE LORD**.

They made... the sacred emblem, out of pure gold and engraved on it... HOLY TO THE LORD (Exodus 39:30).

There is no one as holy as our Lord and Savior Jesus Christ. He is the One who brings true holiness into our lives through His death and resurrection. He declared us holy before God and made us one with Himself, forever cementing us as holy unto the Lord.

PRAY FOR: CHINA

FEBRUARY 12
Leviticus 1, 2; Luke 5

Our word for today is **CATCH**.

*...Jesus said to Simon, "Do not be afraid; from now on you will **catch** men"* (Luke 5:10, NKJV).

Jesus turned fishermen into fishers of men. We, too, are called to be witnesses in this life—to catch those around us with the truth of God's love for every person on earth.

PRAY FOR: CHRISTMAS ISLAND

FEBRUARY 13
Leviticus 3, 4; Luke 6

Our word for today is **MEASURE**.

*"Give, and it will be given to you. A good **measure**, pressed down, shaken together, and running over..."* (Luke 6:38).

Anytime something is built or hung, it must be measured to evaluate the space around it and to evaluate the weight or value of the item. When we build in the Kingdom of God, we can be confident that what we give will be measured honestly and produce results!

PRAY FOR: COCOS (KEELING) ISLANDS

FEBRUARY 14
Leviticus 5, 6, 7; Luke 7, 8

Our thought for today is **GOOD NEWS.**

"... The blind receive sight, the lame walk... and the good news is proclaimed to the poor" (Luke 7:22).

Don't be deceived by the lies of the enemy. He will tell you that God doesn't love you or that He's unhappy with you. Satan doesn't share the good news of Jesus—that you are so loved that God gave His Son for you!

PRAY FOR: COLOMBIA

FEBRUARY 15
Leviticus 8, 9; Luke 9

Our word for today is **APPEAR.**

"... This is what the LORD has commanded you to do, so that the glory of the LORD may appear to you" (Leviticus 9:6).

In today's society, appearance is given high importance, particularly if you want to be successful. Can you imagine how beautiful, intense and empowering it will be when the glory of the Lord appears to all men everywhere? The impact of His glory is way beyond the most beautiful of celebrities!

PRAY FOR: COMOROS

FEBRUARY 16
Leviticus 10, 11; Luke 10

Our word for today is **WORKERS.**

"*. . . The harvest is plentiful, but the workers are few. Ask the* LORD *. . . to send out* **workers** *into his harvest field*" (Luke 10:2).

We are truly blessed living under the grace that we acquired through the Cross of Christ! Not only does He call us to work but He faithfully empowers us to accomplish that work. Ask Him to reveal the harvest fields in your life and follow His leading into them!

PRAY FOR: DEMOCRATIC REPUBLIC OF THE CONGO (KINSHASA)

FEBRUARY 17
Leviticus 12, 13; Luke 11

Our thought for today is **TEACH US.**

. . . one of his disciples said to him, "Lord, **teach us** *to pray, just as John taught his disciples"* (Luke 11:1).

Our disobedience doesn't make God turn His back on us, but it opens a door to teaching opportunities. This doesn't mean God delights in chastening—He delights in us! When He teaches us, it reveals His love for us and our potential for fruitfulness.

PRAY FOR: REPUBLIC OF CONGO (BRAZZAVILLE)

FEBRUARY 18
Leviticus 14, 15; Luke 12

Our word for today is **ACKNOWLEDGE.**

*"... whoever publicly acknowledges me before others, the Son of Man will also **acknowledge** before the angels of God"* (Luke 12:8).

What an amazing promise from a God who loves you! The longing of a child is to be acknowledged publicly before all men. In His infinite wisdom, God provides a way for you to experience His acknowledgment of you as His child.

PRAY FOR: COOK ISLANDS

FEBRUARY 19
Leviticus 16, 17; Luke 13

Our word for today is **ENTER.**

*"Make every effort to **enter** through the narrow door, because many... will try to enter and will not be able to"* (Luke 13:24).

Scripture is filled with opportunities to enter into the promises, rest, blessings and abundance of God. Don't wait! Accept His invitation to enter into all that He has given you today.

PRAY FOR: COSTA RICA

FEBRUARY 20
Leviticus 18, 19; Luke 14

Our word for today is **RESPECT.**

*"Stand up in the presence of the aged, show **respect** for the elderly and revere your God. I am the LORD"* (Leviticus 19:32).
Respect can open doors that dishonor will close. Sometimes it is difficult to respect those who may not respect you in return. However, great blessing and satisfaction come from acting respectfully. Choose to act respectfully, then see how that opens doors for God's intervention in situations and relationships.

PRAY FOR: COTE D'IVOIRE (IVORY COAST)

FEBRUARY 21
Leviticus 20, 21, 22; Luke 15, 16

Our thought for today is **MILK AND HONEY.**

*"... You will possess their land; I will give it to you as an inheritance, a land flowing with **milk and honey**..."* (Leviticus 20:24).
It's interesting to consider the physical mixture of milk and honey. One will calm your stomach and one will stir your energy. When entering new places and situations, God has promised us both peace and excitement!

PRAY FOR: CROATIA

FEBRUARY 22
Leviticus 23, 24; Luke 17

Our word for today is **PRAISING.**

*One of them, when he saw he was healed, came back, **praising** God in a loud voice* (Luke 17:15).

Jehovah-Rapha, the Lord our Healer! Jesus took our sicknesses and our diseases. We are redeemed and healed, and praise flows freely because of that.

PRAY FOR: CUBA

FEBRUARY 23
Leviticus 25, 26; Luke 18

Our word for today is **JUBILEE.**

*"... proclaim liberty throughout the land to all its inhabitants. It shall be a **jubilee** for you..."* (Leviticus 25:10).

Jubilee was a time in Israel when all things were restored to their rightful owners. Our rightful owner is Jesus Christ; He is declaring a jubilee for you today! He's taken you back from the devourer and now is the time to rejoice!

PRAY FOR: CYPRUS

FEBRUARY 24
Leviticus 27; Numbers 1; Luke 19

Our thought for today is **SALVATION HAS COME.**

*Jesus said to him, "Today **salvation has come** to this house..."* (Luke 19:9).

It's already happened. It's already here. There is nothing you need to do but receive the salvation that has come. Take a deep breath and rest in the knowledge that He did the work for you. Salvation is here!

PRAY FOR: CZECH REPUBLIC

FEBRUARY 25
Numbers 2, 3; Luke 20

Our word for today is **COMMANDED.**

*So the Israelites did everything the L*ORD ***commanded... they encamped under their standards...*** (Numbers 2:34).

What a mighty God we serve! He is the Commander of the angels of heaven. He commanded the sea to calm, the lame to walk and the blind to see. His commands are true, honorable and worthy of obedience.

PRAY FOR: DENMARK

FEBRUARY 26
Numbers 4, 5; Luke 21

Our thought for today is **HEAVEN AND EARTH.**

"Heaven and earth will pass away, but my words will never pass away" (Luke 21:33).

The message around the globe is "go green to save Mother Earth." However, we know as believers that there will come a time for heaven and earth to pass away. Spend your time and energy on those things which produce eternal results. Spend time listening to or reading His Word.

PRAY FOR: DJIBOUTI

FEBRUARY 27
Numbers 6, 7; Luke 22

Our thought for today is **BLESS YOU.**

*"'The LORD **bless you** and keep you... be gracious to you... and give you peace'"* (Numbers 6:24-26).

God has blessings for us beyond anything we could ever imagine. Don't allow bitterness or negativity in your life make you miss the blessings He has for you. Your Heavenly Father wants to bless you and even tells you that He will—so accept that promise for your life today!

PRAY FOR: DOMINICA

FEBRUARY 28
Numbers 8, 9, 10; Luke 23, 24

Our thought for today is **POWER.**

*"I am going to send you what my Father has promised... until you have been clothed with **power** from on high"* (Luke 24:49).

You have power as a child of God. Never forget this and never let the enemy tell you differently. He is a deceiver and will tell you that he is greater than any power around you. This is not true! God's power is at work in and through your life.

PRAY FOR: DOMINICAN REPUBLIC

MARCH 1
Numbers 11, 12; John 1

Our word for today is **PROPHETS.**

*"... I wish that all the LORD's people were **prophets** and that the LORD would put his Spirit on them!"* (Numbers 11:29).

There are different kinds of anointing for believers. There is an anointing that heals the sick as you lay hands on them, and there is another anointing which enables you to move in the spoken gift of prophecy, among others.

PRAY FOR: EAST TIMOR (TIMOR-LESTE)

MARCH 2
Numbers 13, 14; John 2

Our word for today is **SIGNS.**

*What Jesus did here in Cana of Galilee was the first of the **signs** through which he revealed his glory; and his disciples believed in him* (John 2:11).

Jesus performed miracles when He was on earth, but He continues to give us signs today. We know that He is alive and at work in our lives! What He did 2,000 years ago, He can do in your life today.

PRAY FOR: ECUADOR

MARCH 3
Numbers 15, 16; John 3

Our thought for today is **KINGDOM OF GOD.**

*Jesus replied, "Very truly I tell you, no one can see the **kingdom of God** unless they are born again"* (John 3:3).

When we look around our world, the kingdoms of this place may depress, anger or frustrate us. Isn't it a wonderful blessing to know that we are not part of those kingdoms? Instead we belong to the King of Kings, who rules the ultimate kingdom for all eternity!

PRAY FOR: EGYPT

MARCH 4
Numbers 17, 18; John 4

Our word for today is **GIFT**.

*"I myself have selected your fellow Levites from among the Israelites as a **gift** to you, dedicated to the LORD..."* (Numbers 18:6).

A gift is freely given, never forced from the giver. Our Lord loves to give gifts to us freely, asking nothing in return, just that we receive. Christ, the original priest, was a gift freely given to us. All God asks in return is that we receive this very special gift.

PRAY FOR: EL SALVADOR

MARCH 5
Numbers 19, 20; John 5

Our word for today is **LIFE**.

*"For just as the Father raises the dead and gives them **life**, even so the Son gives life to whom he is pleased to give it"* (John 5:21).

Through the blood of Jesus, you have a full supply of abundant life—divine, eternal life that sprang forth the moment you were born again!

PRAY FOR: EQUATORIAL GUINEA

MARCH 6
Numbers 21, 22; John 6

Our thought for today is **THE WORK OF GOD.**

Jesus answered, "The work of God is this: to believe in the one he has sent" (John 6:29).

The work of God is simply to believe in Jesus. When you take that step, your whole life is transformed. Your belief and love for Jesus will manifest in every area of your life and enable you to do good work.

PRAY FOR: ERITREA

MARCH 7
Numbers 23, 24, 25; John 7, 8

Our thought for today is **OWN ACCORD.**

*'Even if Balak gave me all the silver and gold in his palace, I could not do anything of my **own accord**, good or bad, to go beyond the command of the LORD—and I must say only what the LORD says'?* (Numbers 24:13).

The freedom to choose is such a wonderful blessing and at the same time a heavy burden. Of our own accord, we choose daily whom we will serve and how we will act.

PRAY FOR: ESTONIA

MARCH 8
Numbers 26, 27; John 9

Our word for today is **SHEPHERD.**

*"... the LORD'S people will not be like sheep without a **shepherd**"* (Numbers 27:17).

Jehovah-Raah is another name God goes by in the Old Testament which tells us that the Lord is our Shepherd. We are not like lost sheep; we have a Shepherd, and He leads us to green pastures!

PRAY FOR: ETHIOPIA

MARCH 9
Numbers 28, 29; John 10

Our word for today is **SHEEP.**

*When he has brought out all his own, he goes on ahead of them, and his **sheep** follow him because they know his voice* (John 10:4).

Just as Jesus is our Shepherd, sometimes we are also called to feed the sheep around us. The Lord really dealt with me on this. He said, "If you're going to feed sheep, you're going to have to have the love that God has."

PRAY FOR: FALKLAND ISLANDS

MARCH 10
Numbers 30, 31; John 11

Our word for today is **RESURRECTION.**

*"... I am the **resurrection** and the life. The one who believes in me will live..."* (John 11:25).

It is very comforting to know that there is life after death and hope for seeing loved ones who have gone before us. Because Christ was resurrected, now we, too, can see beyond the grave.

PRAY FOR: FAROE ISLANDS

MARCH 11
Numbers 32, 33; John 12

Our thought for today is **FOLLOW WHOLEHEARTEDLY.**

*... Caleb... and Joshua... followed the LORD **wholeheartedly*** (Numbers 32:12).

God only asks that our hearts be pure and that we be willing to follow His guidance. If we meet those requirements, our boundaries are limitless, and we can expect to perform tremendous feats in our world.

PRAY FOR: FIJI

MARCH 12
Numbers 34, 35; John 13

Our word for today is **REFUGE**.

*"Six of the towns... will be cities of **refuge**, to which a person... may flee..."* (Numbers 35:6).

What mercy and grace we have been given from God! When we need to hide and run, even then He provides a place away from the commotion and cares of this life. He provides a refuge in the storm.

PRAY FOR: FINLAND

MARCH 13
Numbers 36; Deuteronomy 1; John 14

Our thought for today is **GREATER THINGS**.

*"... whoever believes in me will do... even **greater things** than these, because I am going to the Father"* (John 14:12).

Greater things imply moving forward or moving up. In our Christian walk, we continue to move forward into the greater things of God... into a greater understanding of His great love for us... into a deeper love for those around us... into greater things.

PRAY FOR: FRANCE

MARCH 14
Deuteronomy 2, 3, 4; John 15, 16

Our word for today is **TRUTH.**

*". . . the Spirit of truth . . . will guide you into all the **truth** . . . and he will tell you what is yet to come"* (John 16:13).

The Holy Spirit wants to glorify Christ in your life. He wants to confirm the truth of God's Word to you and give you power for service that furthers God's Kingdom. The Spirit will always guide you in truth.

PRAY FOR: FRENCH GUIANA

MARCH 15
Deuteronomy 5, 6; John 17

Our thought for today is **I AM THE LORD.**

"I am the LORD your God, who brought you out of Egypt, out of the land of slavery" (Deuteronomy 5:6).

What a declaration! I AM. There is no other who can claim these words but our Lord. He is the One Who created the universe. He is the One Who died to save all of humanity. He is the One Who will return and establish His Kingdom on this earth.

PRAY FOR: FRENCH POLYNESIA

MARCH 16
Deuteronomy 7, 8; John 18

Our word for today is **TREASURED.**

*The L*ORD *your God has chosen you... to be his people, his treasured possession* (Deuteronomy 7:6).

In the US and the West, we are blessed with many possessions. However, how many of our possessions do we truly treasure? Most likely, what we treasure are people or the intangible things, like time. Know today that God treasures you above all other things in His creation.

PRAY FOR: FRENCH SOUTHERN TERRITORIES

MARCH 17
Deuteronomy 9, 10; John 19

Our word for today is **LOVE.**

*...walk in all his ways... love him... the L*ORD *your God...* (Deuteronomy 10:12, ESV).

It is when you are moving in the love of God that you can be most productive. If you don't have a good root system in love, productivity will fall away. When your roots go deep in love of the Father, you're going to bear fruit.

PRAY FOR: GABON

MARCH 18
Deuteronomy 11, 12; John 20

Our word for today is **PEACE**.

*Again Jesus said, "**Peace** be with you! As the Father has sent me, I am sending you"* (John 20:21).

Often times we don't experience peace. If you want to have the peace of God, start thanking Him for each situation and person in your life. We are equipped with what we need to experience peace.

PRAY FOR: GAMBIA

MARCH 19
Deuteronomy 13, 14; John 21

Our thought for today is **HOLD FAST**.

*"It is the LORD your God you must follow... Keep his commands... and **hold fast** to him"* (Deuteronomy 13:4).

Often, we experience deep levels of grief and frustration, but if we hold fast to God's promises, any situation can be altered! Cling to Him and trust that He will guide you through each and every situation you face.

PRAY FOR: GEORGIA

MARCH 20
Deuteronomy 15, 16; Acts 1

Our word for today is **ALIVE.**

*After his suffering, he presented himself to them and gave many convincing proofs that he was **alive**...* (Acts 1:3).

I can't begin to imagine the experience of seeing Jesus, who was once dead, now alive and standing in my presence! How shocking and exhilarating it must have been for the disciples, to see the power of God transform the very being of Jesus, from death to life.

PRAY FOR: GERMANY

MARCH 21
Deuteronomy 17, 18, 19; Acts 2, 3

Our word for today is **INHERITANCE.**

*The... tribe of Levi... shall live on the... offerings presented to the L*ORD*, for that is their **inheritance*** (Deuteronomy 18:1).

In this world of 401K and IRA accounts, isn't it comforting to know that the Father has planned for our inheritance? Rather than leaving us the inheritance of the old Adam, He ensured through Christ that we would inherit all that His Only Son inherits.

PRAY FOR: GHANA

MARCH 22
Deuteronomy 20, 21; Acts 4

Our word for today is **MESSAGE**.

*But many who heard the **message** believed; so the number of men who believed grew to about five thousand* (Acts 4:4).

The message of the Cross is so powerful and transforming, we only need to share it. Let the message do the work of changing hearts and minds. Our job is simply to share it.

PRAY FOR: GIBRALTAR

MARCH 23
Deuteronomy 22, 23; Acts 5

Our thought for today is **MIRACULOUS SIGNS**.

*The apostles were performing many **miraculous signs** and wonders among the people...* (Acts 5:12, NLT).

Did you know that you are filled with miracle-working power? When you're filled with the Holy Spirit, you are filled with virtue, and virtue is miracle-working power. It wasn't given just to be in you; it is to flow through you and to touch others!

PRAY FOR: GREAT BRITAIN

MARCH 24
Deuteronomy 24, 25; Acts 6

Our word for today is **BLESS**.

> *"When you are harvesting... and you overlook a sheaf... leave it for... the widow, so that the* LORD... *may* **bless** *you..."* (Deuteronomy 24:19).

The blessing of the Lord is a long lasting and amazing gift. Even today, thousands of years after declaring Abraham blessed, we still see the blessings of the Lord continue to fall upon the nation of Israel.

PRAY FOR: GREECE

MARCH 25
Deuteronomy 26, 27; Acts 7

Our word for today is **REJOICE**.

> *... you shall* **rejoice** *in all the good things the* LORD *your God has given to you and your household* (Deuteronomy 26:11).

Whatever it is that you need, rejoice! Jesus has already given you the provision: His Word! He came to give life in His abundance, and He's already given you your freedom. Now you just need to take it.

PRAY FOR: GREENLAND

MARCH 26
Deuteronomy 28, 29; Acts 8

Our word for today is **SCRIPTURE.**

*Then Philip began with that very passage of **Scripture** and told him the good news about Jesus* (Acts 8:35).

The more you put the Word in your heart, the more it will bring healing to you. Take Scripture as you would your daily vitamins; read the words, think about them, say them out loud.

PRAY FOR: GRENADA

MARCH 27
Deuteronomy 30, 31; Acts 9

Our thought for today is **NEVER LEAVE YOU.**

*"... the LORD your God goes with you; he will **never leave you** nor forsake you"* (Deuteronomy 31:6).

I can't always immediately see the hand of God in everything that happens to me. Sometimes it takes me a while. It takes renewing my mind with the Word, being reminded or repenting. But I know that God will never leave me, and He can take over any situation I face.

PRAY FOR: GUADELOUPE

MARCH 28
Deuteronomy 32, 33, 34; Acts 10, 11

Our word for today is **FAVORITISM.**

"... God does not show favoritism but accepts from every nation the one who fears him and does what is right" (Acts 10:34-35).

When I study the Word, God shows me that He doesn't take sides; He doesn't show favoritism. We are all His children. He loved the people of Baal as much as He loved the Israelites. He wants them to see that He is the true and living God. He loves the world!

PRAY FOR: GUAM

MARCH 29
Joshua 1, 2; Acts 12

Our word for today is **PROMISED.**

"I will give you every place where you set your foot, as I promised Moses" (Joshua 1:3).

God's promises of favor found in the Word will miraculously transform your life! Only the Word of God and the promises we find within, have the power to alter attitudes and change hearts.

PRAY FOR: GUATEMALA

MARCH 30
Joshua 3, 4; Acts 13

Our word for today is **LISTEN.**

"...Come here and listen to the words of the LORD" (Joshua 3:9).

God has given us the Word to bring life and to bring health. We have the heavenly prescription for good health. Attend to the Word by listening to it (which implies obeying it), reading it, and meditating on it.

PRAY FOR: GUINEA

MARCH 31
Joshua 5, 6; Acts 14

Our word for today is **DOOR.**

...they...reported all that God had done through them and how he had opened a door of faith to the Gentiles (Acts 14:27).

An "open-door policy" was a corporate term thrown around a few years back. It indicated that a boss was always available to be approached by his employees. Through the work on the Cross, God gave us an eternal, open door, with unlimited access to Him and all His benefits!

PRAY FOR: GUINEA-BISSAU

APRIL 1
Joshua 7, 8:1-15; Acts 15

Our word for today is **CONSECRATE**.

"...Consecrate yourselves in preparation for tomorrow; for this is what the LORD, the God of Israel, says..." (Joshua 7:13).

It is a wonderful thing to be living under the new covenant of grace! Jesus consecrated us to God, a treasure for Himself. Today, turn your eyes upon Jesus and receive the consecration and cleansing He has provided.

PRAY FOR: GUYANA

APRIL 2
Joshua 8:16-35, 9; Acts 16

Our thought for today is **BOOK OF THE LAW**.

...Joshua read all the words of the law...written in the Book of the Law (Joshua 8:34).

We know that every book of the Bible, in some way or another, reflects the truth of Jesus and God's love for man. Today, let's believe together that Jesus will reveal Himself to you through the Truth found in the books of the law.

PRAY FOR: HAITI

APRIL 3
Joshua 10, 11; Acts 17

Our word for today is **CHRIST.**

*. . . Christ had to suffer and rise again from the dead, and saying, "This Jesus whom I preach to you is the **Christ**"* (Acts 17:3, NKJV).

For generations, the Jews watched and waited for the appearance of the Messiah, the Christ. How sad that when He walked among them, only a portion of them recognized Him. Let's not make the same mistake. Instead, spend every day seeing Jesus in the Scriptures, in ourselves and in the world around us.

PRAY FOR: HOLY SEE

APRIL 4
Joshua 12, 13, 14; Acts 18, 19

Our word for today is **VIGOROUS.**

*"I am still as strong today as the day Moses sent me out; I'm just as **vigorous** to go out to battle now as I was then"* (Joshua 14:11).

One of the many promises of God is having our strength renewed and restored. His desire is for us to be vigorous every day and live our lives to their fullest.

PRAY FOR: HONDURAS

APRIL 5
Joshua 15, 16; Acts 20

Our word for today is **RACE.**

*...I consider my life worth nothing to me; my only aim is to finish the **race** and complete the task...* (Acts 20:24).

Don't stop! As long as you are on this earth, continue to run the race you started. You may have been running for a long time or just recently started the race, either way...don't stop! Aim to finish the race.

PRAY FOR: HONG KONG

APRIL 6
Joshua 17, 18; Acts 21

Our thought for today is **AN INHERITANCE.**

*...Joshua gave them **an inheritance**...according to the LORD's command* (Joshua 17:4).

Ask God to reveal the inheritance He has already given you. You have already received your inheritance! Knowing this will make you victorious and give you supernatural ability to prosper.

PRAY FOR: HUNGARY

APRIL 7
Joshua 19, 20; Acts 22

Our word for today is **WITNESS.**

*"... hear words from his mouth. You will be his **witness** to all people of what you have seen and heard"* (Acts 22:14–15).

A witness is someone who testifies of what he knows. Be open to talk with others who are seeking God. Your words are important and can lead others to God's Word just as you were led!

PRAY FOR: ICELAND

APRIL 8
Joshua 21, 22; Acts 23

Our word for today is **ALTAR.**

*"... do not rebel... by building an **altar**... other than the **altar** of the LORD..."* (Joshua 22:19).

For many people, the foot of the Cross is now the altar of the Lord. At any time, on any day, you can bow your head, get on your knees and pray before the altar of the sacrifice of the Lamb of God. His death on the Cross was the final sacrifice, the finished work to end all other sacrifice.

PRAY FOR: INDIA

APRIL 9
Joshua 23, 24; Acts 24

Our thought for today is **STRIVE ALWAYS.**

*So I **strive always** to keep my conscience clear before God and man* (Acts 24:16).

I always say that if you're not sure, it's best not to do it. We can always work to keep our conscience clear, asking God for direction in the areas where we strive to be more like Christ in our actions.

PRAY FOR: INDONESIA

APRIL 10
Judges 1, 2; Acts 25

Our word for today is **POSSESSION.**

*The LORD was with the men of Judah. They took **possession** of the hill country...* (Judges 1:19).

Ownership is a very empowering position in which to exist. When you are confident of your ownership, you don't hesitate to make full use of what you own. God provided everything we need through Christ's work on the Cross: redemption, healing, favor and hope. It's time to take possession of what you already own.

PRAY FOR: IRAN (ISLAMIC REPUBLIC OF)

APRIL 11
Judges 3, 4, 5; Acts 26, 27

Our thought for today is **WHAT I AM.**

*"... I pray to God that ... all who are listening to me today may become **what I am**, except for these chains"* (Acts 26:29).

Reading this statement from Paul, one would almost think he was an arrogant man. But no, he was a man who understood all that Christ had made him to be and that without the saving grace of the Cross, he was nothing. Today, purpose in your heart to be all that I AM has made you to be!

PRAY FOR: IRAQ

APRIL 12
Judges 6, 7; Acts 28

Our word for today is **KINGDOM.**

*He proclaimed the **kingdom** of God ... with all boldness and without hindrance!* (Acts 28:31).

It's important to never forget we are not of this world. We truly don't belong here and will never completely fit. We are servants of another Kingdom. So don't get too comfortable here!

PRAY FOR: IRELAND

APRIL 13
Judges 8, 9; Romans 1

Our word for today is **CALLED.**

*And you also are among those Gentiles who are **called** to belong to Jesus Christ* (Romans 1:6).

I love receiving phone calls from close friends, don't you? Of course, the calling of the Lord is so much deeper and more intimate than a phone call from a friend. Yet in its most simplistic form, how wonderful to receive this unique call from our friend, Jesus.

PRAY FOR: ISRAEL

APRIL 14
Judges 10, 11; Romans 2

Our word for today is **HONOR.**

*. . . glory, **honor** and peace for everyone who does good: first for the Jew, then for the Gentile* (Romans 2:10).

It's sad to say, but it seems that the understanding of honor is getting lost in a world that is driven by equal rights. Honoring those who deserve it, like parents, veterans and pastors, can bring a sense of completeness and peace. Remember to honor those around you who are deserving of it.

PRAY FOR: ITALY

APRIL 15
Judges 12, 13; Romans 3

Our thought for today is **DEDICATED.**

... the boy is to be a Nazirite, **dedicated** *to God from the womb...* (Judges 13:5).

One of the great things about dedication is that you can always rededicate! Choose today to rededicate yourself to the call God originally placed on your life. Rededicate yourself to love others around you as Christ has loved you. Rededicate yourself to put Christ first in all that you do!

PRAY FOR: JAMAICA

APRIL 16
Judges 14, 15; Romans 4

Our word for today is **POWERFUL.**

The Spirit of the LORD came **powerfully** *upon him so that he tore the lion apart with his bare hands...* (Judges 14:6).

The Holy Spirit creates and gives life, just as He created new spiritual life within you when you were born again. The Spirit dwells with us; at times it may be manifested powerfully in your life.

PRAY FOR: JAPAN

APRIL 17
Judges 16, 17; Romans 5

Our word for today is **GOD'S LOVE.**

*...**God's love** has been poured out into our hearts through the Holy Spirit...*(Romans 5:5).

God comforts and pours love out on all believers through the Holy Spirit. The Holy Spirit dwells with you and exists to comfort, direct, convict and empower you, just as Jesus would if He were physically present.

PRAY FOR: JORDAN

APRIL 18
Judges 18, 19, 20; Romans 6, 7

Our word for today is **NEW.**

*...we have been released from the law so that we serve in the **new** way of the Spirit...*(Romans 7:6).

You live a new lifestyle when you enter a relationship with God. This new way of the Spirit doesn't consist of striving to be good, but rather it is allowing the powerful, perfect life of Jesus to be in complete control.

PRAY FOR: KAZAKHSTAN

APRIL 19
Judges 21; Ruth 1; Romans 8

Our thought for today is **MY GOD.**

... *"Where you go I will go... Your people will be my people and your God **my** God"* (Ruth 1:16).

Intimacy with God is such a wonderful thing! He's not just GOD but He is MY GOD. Mine to spend time with, mine to cry with, mine to share with others and mine to hold onto during difficult times. Mine.

PRAY FOR: KENYA

APRIL 20
Ruth 2, 3; Romans 9

Our word for today is **LOVED.**

... *"I will call them 'my people' who are not my people; and... '**my** loved one' who is not my loved one"* (Romans 9:25).

The love of God is greater than anything this world can offer. God's love has chased you through generations and across nations. His love was before time began and will continue throughout eternity. This amazing love of His has been given to you today. You are loved by the only One in the universe Who loves perfectly.

PRAY FOR: KIRIBATI

APRIL 21
Ruth 4; 1 Samuel 1; Romans 10

Our word for today is **GRANTED**.

*I prayed for this child, and the LORD has **granted** me what I asked of him* (1 Samuel 1:27).

Just as Hannah's prayer for a child was granted, the Lord wants to give you what you ask of Him, too. When we expect His blessings in our lives, it activates our faith. Believe today that He will grant what you ask of Him!

PRAY FOR: KOREA, DEMOCRATIC PEOPLE'S REP. (NORTH KOREA)

APRIL 22
1 Samuel 2, 3; Romans 11

Our word for today is **ROCK**.

*"There is no one holy like the LORD; there is no one besides you; there is no **Rock** like our God"* (1 Samuel 2:2).

Living by the Rocky Mountains has given me an appreciation for truly large rocks. Yet, we know that Christ is a Rock that is larger, stronger, and unable to be moved or broken beyond anything the Rocky Mountains contain. The Rock of Christ is where our faith sits and where we can be secure, knowing He will never be shaken.

PRAY FOR: KOREA, REPUBLIC OF (SOUTH KOREA)

APRIL 23
1 Samuel 4, 5; Romans 12

Our word for today is **TRANSFORMED.**

*Do not conform to the pattern of this world, but be **transformed** by the renewing of your mind . . .* (Romans 12:2).

If you find yourself thinking negative thoughts about the people who have hurt you, then mentally separate yourself from those thoughts and renew your mind! God will transform your thinking when you allow Him to renew your mind.

PRAY FOR: KOSOVO

APRIL 24
1 Samuel 6, 7; Romans 13

Our thought for today is **SERVED THE LORD.**

*So the Israelites put away their Baals and Ashtoreths, and **served the LORD** only* (1 Samuel 7:4).

One of the greatest examples of servant leadership is found when Jesus washed the feet of His disciples. He made it clear that the best way we can serve the Lord is to serve others. Consider today, whom would God have you serve? Who around you is in need?

PRAY FOR: KUWAIT

APRIL 25
1 Samuel 8, 9, 10; Romans 14, 15

Our word for today is **PEACE**.

*For the kingdom of God is not a matter of eating and drinking, but of righteousness, **peace** and joy in the Holy Spirit* (Romans 14:17).

Peace is both a promise to the believer and evidence of living in the Kingdom of God while being present on this earth. When we are at peace, we crack the door to a dimension that is not of this world. Through Christ, we can live in peace even when surrounded by chaos.

PRAY FOR: KYRGYZSTAN

APRIL 26
1 Samuel 11, 12; Romans 16

Our thought for today is **FEAR THE LORD**.

*"But be sure to **fear the LORD** and serve him faithfully with all your heart..."* (1 Samuel 12:24).

Fear of the Lord can be a difficult concept in our modern English language. Fear is so often equated with a negative connotation. However, reverence and respect, never go out of style. If the word fear is problematic for you, use revere and respect... even, deeply honor.

PRAY FOR: LAO, PEOPLE'S DEMOCRATIC REPUBLIC

APRIL 27
1 Samuel 13, 14; 1 Corinthians 1

Our word for today is **STRONG**.

*He will keep you **strong** to the end so that you will be free from all blame on the day when our LORD Jesus Christ returns* (1 Corinthians 1:8, NLT).

We all have moments of weakness and failure, but God loves us even at our worst. God takes over when we are weak. He knows exactly what we need, and it is through Christ that we are made strong—even in our moments of weakness!

PRAY FOR: LATVIA

APRIL 28
1 Samuel 15, 16; 1 Corinthians 2

Our thought for today is **THE SPIRIT SEARCHES**.

*... The **Spirit searches** all things, even the deep things of God* (1 Corinthians 2:10).

How comforting it is to know that the Holy Spirit searches all things for us! You don't have to strive, stress or worry because you can rest knowing that the Holy Spirit will bring to you all that you need to see and know.

PRAY FOR: LEBANON

APRIL 29
1 Samuel 17, 18; 1 Corinthians 3

Our word for today is **TRIUMPHED.**

*So David **triumphed** over the Philistine with a sling and a stone; without a sword...* (1 Samuel 17:50).

Are there circumstances in your life where it is time to see a victory? Don't be deceived into looking at the natural to triumph over your situation. Remember, with God on your side, all it may take is a stone and a sling.

PRAY FOR: LESOTHO

APRIL 30
1 Samuel 19, 20; 1 Corinthians 4

Our word for today is **POWER.**

*For the kingdom of God is not a matter of talk but of **power*** (1 Corinthians 4:20).

Have you ever noticed how much the enemy likes to talk? He speaks to you of doubt, fear and unbelief. Don't be fooled by his words; instead remember that the power of God has called you out of darkness and into HIS light!

PRAY FOR: LIBERIA

MAY 1
1 Samuel 21, 22; 1 Corinthians 5

Our word for today is **SAFE.**

"... *don't be afraid. The man who wants to kill you is trying to kill me too. You will be **safe** with me*" (1 Samuel 22:23).

One of the deepest needs of mankind is to feel safe and secure. Seek to spend time with the One Who has promised to keep you and your loved ones safe in a world full of trouble.

PRAY FOR: LIBYA

MAY 2
1 Samuel 23, 24, 25; 1 Corinthians 6, 7

Our word for today is **JUSTIFIED.**

... *you were washed, you were sanctified, you were **justified** in the name of the Lord Jesus Christ...* (1 Corinthians 6:11).

To be wrongly accused is a horrible experience and, sometimes, to be justifiably accused is impossible to defend. We were sinners, rightfully accused and sentenced. However, because of the deep and abiding love of our Father, Another took our place! Christ exchanged our condemnation for His just standing with God, forever sealing our fate as justified, cleansed and sanctified.

PRAY FOR: LIECHTENSTEIN

MAY 3
1 Samuel 26, 27; 1 Corinthians 8

Our thought for today is **KNOWN BY GOD.**

*But whoever loves God is **known by God*** (1 Corinthians 8:3).

Who are the people in your life that really know you—people who know the good, the bad and the ugly, not just the pretty parts? How much more your Father God knows you and loves you! How wonderful to be known by the Creator of the universe! How wonderful to be considered of consequence to Him!

PRAY FOR: LITHUANIA

MAY 4
1 Samuel 28, 29; 1 Corinthians 9

Our word for today is **PREACH.**

*For when I **preach** the gospel, I cannot boast, since I am compelled to preach . . .* (1 Corinthians 9:16).

There is a time to preach, it's true. There is a time to set aside all constraints and preach the truth of salvation through Jesus Christ! Is it your time?

PRAY FOR: LUXEMBOURG

MAY 5
1 Samuel 30, 31; 1 Corinthians 10

Our thought for today is **STRENGTH IN THE LORD.**

*... David found **strength in the LORD** his God* (1 Samuel 30:6).

When you start acknowledging Christ's strength in you, you'll find out that you can do all things through Him. Like David, we can find strength in the Lord that will empower us to get through even the most difficult trials.

PRAY FOR: MACAU

MAY 6
2 Samuel 1, 2; 1 Corinthians 11

Our word for today is **KINDNESS.**

*"May the LORD now show you **kindness** and faithfulness... because you have done this"* (2 Samuel 2:6).

One of the most enduring and underappreciated character traits is kindness. A kind person can open doors of favor. They can begin discussions with opposing parties and can soften even the hardest of hearts.

PRAY FOR: MACEDONIA, REPUBLIC OF

MAY 7
2 Samuel 3, 4; 1 Corinthians 12

Our word for today is **BAPTIZED.**

*For we were all **baptized** by one Spirit so as to form one body—whether Jews or Gentiles, slave or free...* (1 Corinthians 12:13).

When you were born again, you were baptized into the Body of Christ. With this baptism, the Holy Spirit lives in you to give you God's life and presence. And as you enter the Body of Christ, you find your place with other believers in the Body.

PRAY FOR: MADAGASCAR

MAY 8
2 Samuel 5, 6; 1 Corinthians 13

Our thought for today is **FAITH, HOPE AND LOVE.**

*And now these three remain: **faith, hope and love**. But the greatest of these is love* (1 Corinthians 13:13).

Faith, hope and love must coexist. Faith works by love and hope increases faith. They must work together to be productive. We are rooted and grounded in love, and it is important that we never lose it.

PRAY FOR: MALAWI

MAY 9
2 Samuel 7, 8, 9; 1 Corinthians 14, 15

Our word for today is **VICTORY.**

*But thanks be to God! He gives us the **victory** through our Lord Jesus Christ* (1 Corinthians 15:57).

We are victorious through Christ our Savior! And when we take Jesus with us, no matter what circumstances we face, we will win. We can rejoice today because of the victory that we have already been given through Jesus!

PRAY FOR: MALAYSIA

MAY 10
2 Samuel 10, 11; 1 Corinthians 16

Our word for today is **BE STRONG.**

*"Be **strong**, and let us fight bravely for our people… The LORD will do what is good in his sight"* (2 Samuel 10:12).

We can be grateful that our strength comes from the Lord. He has promised us that when we are weak, He will give us the strength we need. So, if you are feeling weak or discouraged today, take hope in His strength. Be strong in your faith!

PRAY FOR: MALDIVES

MAY 11
2 Samuel 12, 13; 2 Corinthians 1

Our word for today is **OWNERSHIP**.

> ...*God... set his seal of **ownership** on us, and put his Spirit in our hearts as a deposit*... (2 Corinthians 1:21–22).

You are His. He has claimed you and called you by name. Never believe the feelings of abandonment or loneliness that the enemy brings your way. You are His.

PRAY FOR: MALI

MAY 12
2 Samuel 14, 15; 2 Corinthians 2

Our word for today is **DWELLING**.

> "*... Take the ark of God back into the city... If I find favor in the LORD's eyes, He will... let me see it and his **dwelling** place again*" (2 Samuel 15:25).

For generations God abided within the Ark of the Covenant. His presence was a beacon and a promise of things to come. We now live in the time He promised and His spirit dwells in us. We have become His dwelling place.

PRAY FOR: MALTA

MAY 13
2 Samuel 16, 17; 2 Corinthians 3

Our word for today is **FREEDOM.**

. . . where the Spirit of the LORD is, there is freedom (2 Corinthians 3:17).

Do you ever get depressed, and no matter how hard you try to break free, the dreariness lingers? Stop fighting to break free—you are free! You are the Bride of Christ, and in that identity, there is freedom!

PRAY FOR: MARSHALL ISLANDS

MAY 14
2 Samuel 18, 19; 2 Corinthians 4

Our word for today is **GRACE.**

. . . grace . . . may cause thanksgiving to overflow to the glory of God (2 Corinthians 4:15).

Because of His death, we enjoy the benefits of God's grace and mercy, we enjoy His very presence, and we call ourselves "Christians." His grace covers us, and we give overflowing thanks because of that.

PRAY FOR: MARTINIQUE

MAY 15
2 Samuel 20, 21; 2 Corinthians 5

Our word for today is **OATH.**

*The king spared Mephibosheth son of Jonathan... because of the **oath** before the LORD...* (2 Samuel 21:7).

In the U.S., when we go before a judge to give our testimony, it requires an oath, an agreement that we will tell the truth, regardless of how it makes ourselves or others appear. An oath is not something to be entered into lightly and never should it be easily broken.

PRAY FOR: MAURITANIA

MAY 16
2 Samuel 22, 23, 24; 2 Corinthians 6, 7

Our thought for today is **DAY OF SALVATION.**

*For He says, "In the time of my favor I heard you, and in the **day of salvation** I helped you."* (2 Corinthians 6:2).

Today is a new day, the past has been washed away. Today, walk in the salvation that Christ bestowed upon you through His work on the Cross. You have been saved from the consequences of sin and given a new life of hope, peace and joy!

PRAY FOR: MAURITIUS

MAY 17
1 Kings 1, 2; 2 Corinthians 8

Our word for today is **EXCEL**.

*...**excel** in everything—in faith, in speech, in knowledge, in complete earnestness and in...love...* (2 Corinthians 8:7).

Don't settle for the lesser things in life. Don't let yourself be satisfied with a little when you know that God has so much more for you. Reach out and push yourself toward the goals He set for you. Don't give up, give in or give out!

PRAY FOR: MAYOTTE

MAY 18
1 Kings 3, 4; 2 Corinthians 9

Our word for today is **DISCERNING**.

*"So give your servant a **discerning** heart...to distinguish between right and wrong..."* (1 Kings 3:9).

Have you ever felt the gentle pressing of unquietness within yourself? Have you looked at your situation and all seems right...and yet there is a lack of peace within you? Listen to that quiet voice of discernment. It's a gift from God to guide you through your day.

PRAY FOR: MEXICO

MAY 19
1 Kings 5, 6; 2 Corinthians 10

Our word for today is **DIVINE**.

*The weapons we fight with are not the weapons of the world... they have **divine** power to demolish strongholds* (2 Corinthians 10:4).

It is hard to comprehend the divine. We are bound to this world and the natural elements around us. Yet, there is something beyond our experience and outside the dimension we live in, something divine and holy. He has given us this divine power that goes beyond the natural and into the supernatural, impacting realms beyond our own!

PRAY FOR: MICRONESIA, FEDERAL STATE OF

MAY 20
1 Kings 7, 8; 2 Corinthians 11

Our thought for today is **SINGLED OUT**.

*"For you **singled** [Israel] **out** from all the nations of the world to be your own inheritance..."* (1 Kings 8:53).

As a child, I remember the feeling of being chosen to participate on a team. It was so special to be one of the first ones chosen and so humiliating when I was chosen last! Do you know that you have been singled out and chosen by God? He isn't waiting until you are last to pick you. He chose you before the creation of the world! You have been singled out.

PRAY FOR: MOLDOVA, REPUBLIC OF

MAY 21
1 Kings 9, 10; 2 Corinthians 12

Our word for today is **WISDOM.**

*King Solomon was greater in riches and **wisdom** than all the other kings of the earth* (1 Kings 10:23).

When given the opportunity, Solomon asked for wisdom above all else. As a result, God blessed him with riches and peace. Let's follow Solomon's example today and ask for wisdom from God for all our struggles and trials.

PRAY FOR: MONACO

MAY 22
1 Kings 11, 12; 2 Corinthians 13

Our word for today is **RESTORATION.**

*…Strive for full **restoration**, encourage one another, be of one mind, live in peace. And the God of love and peace will be with you* (2 Corinthians 13:11).

True and full restoration in an estranged relationship can bring about an even closer relationship than before the estrangement. When you consider all that Christ did so that we could be restored to God, it creates a gratefulness that didn't exist prior to the restoration. What relationships in your life need to be fully restored? Will you surrender those over to God today?

PRAY FOR: MONGOLIA

MAY 23
1 Kings 13, 14, 15; Galatians 1, 2

Our thought for today is **RESCUE US.**

. . . the Lord Jesus Christ . . . gave himself for our sins to rescue us from the present evil age . . . (Galatians 1:3–4).

We have a merciful heavenly Father who came to our rescue simply because He loves His children! He is able to deliver us from all circumstances—even the ones that seem impossible. Thank you, God, for rescuing us!

PRAY FOR: MONTENEGRO

MAY 24
1 Kings 16, 17; Galatians 3

Our word for today is **LIFE.**

". . . LORD my God, let this boy's life return to him!" The LORD heard Elijah's cry, and the boy . . . lived (1 Kings 17:21–22).

Your life is a very precious gift from God, not something to be wasted or squandered. His desire for you is to live your life to the fullest and produce a bountiful harvest. His very breath was breathed into Adam and continues to flow through you today. Grab hold of all that life has to offer!

PRAY FOR: MONTSERRAT

MAY 25
1 Kings 18, 19; Galatians 4

Our word for today is **STILL SMALL VOICE.**

> . . . *the* LORD *was not in the fire; and after the fire a **still small voice*** (1 Kings 19:12, NKJV).

We are surrounded by so many voices—the news, people, circumstances—and they're all so loud. God whispers. Learn to hear His whisper, so sweet and so important. It means I have to tune out all of the static around me and say, "God, talk to me. I'm listening."

PRAY FOR: MOROCCO

MAY 26
1 Kings 20, 21; Galatians 5

Our thought for today is **I WILL DELIVER.**

> "... *I will deliver this vast army into your hands, and you will know that I am the* LORD" (1 Kings 20:28).

The faster this world moves, the greater demand there is to have everything delivered directly into our hands. Online shopping has changed the concept of quick delivery. However, as fast as second-day service is, nothing can beat the God of heaven making a special delivery to meet your need. What do you need to order from Him today?

PRAY FOR: MOZAMBIQUE

MAY 27
1 Kings 22; 2 Kings 1; Galatians 6

Our word for today is **SHARE.**

*... the one who receives instruction in the word should **share** all good things with their instructor* (Galatians 6:6).

When the Holy Spirit shares unique insight and revelation with you, take the time to seek His wisdom and direction. He may be asking you to share that insight with others.

PRAY FOR: MYANMAR, BURMA

MAY 28
2 Kings 2, 3; Ephesians 1

Our word for today is **REVELATION.**

*I keep asking that the God of our LORD Jesus Christ... may give you the Spirit of wisdom and **revelation**...* (Ephesians 1:17).

Pray and seek God's revelation in every situation. Personal prayer brings understanding. And when you receive a clear understanding of the situation, you will conduct yourself according to God's revelation.

PRAY FOR: NAMIBIA

MAY 29
2 Kings 4, 5; Ephesians 2

Our thought for today is **RAISED US UP.**

*And God **raised us up** with Christ and seated us with him in the heavenly realms in Christ Jesus* (Ephesians 2:6).

We are raised up out of the trials, struggles and defeats of this world! Isn't that good news? We are no longer subject to the rulers of this kingdom on earth. Instead, we are subjects to a higher being Who abides in heavenly places.

PRAY FOR: NAURU

MAY 30
2 Kings 6, 7, 8; Ephesians 3, 4

Our thought for today is **DON'T BE AFRAID.**

*"**Don't be afraid**... Those who are with us are more than those who are with them"* (2 Kings 6:16).

If you are going to get things done for God you must be aggressive. You can't stand around and be afraid of circumstances. You must act with the knowledge that the Lord is your Helper. Don't be afraid!

PRAY FOR: NEPAL

MAY 31
2 Kings 9, 10; Ephesians 5

Our word for today is **SING**.

*Speaking to one another with psalms, hymns, and songs from the Spirit. **Sing** and make music from your heart to the Lord* (Ephesians 5:19).

Is it time to sing a new song to the Lord? David, a man after God's own heart, discovered the secret release that comes from singing a new song to God. Maybe it's time for you to stop repeating the same old verses and let the Holy Spirit lead you into new levels of praise!

PRAY FOR: NETHERLANDS

JUNE 1
2 Kings 11, 12; Ephesians 6

Our word for today is **WHOLEHEARTEDLY**.

*Serve **wholeheartedly**, as if you were serving the Lord, not people* (Ephesians 6:7).

Half measures will only get you half of the reward. Stop accepting half of what God has for you. Step out and wholeheartedly follow His calling on your life. Isn't it time to see Him fully manifest?

PRAY FOR: NETHERLANDS ANTILLES

JUNE 2
2 Kings 13, 14; Philippians 1

Our word for today is **PREACHED**.

*...The important thing is that...Christ is **preached**. And because of this I rejoice* (Philippians 1:18).

We need to rejoice whenever we hear that the gospel has been preached. Maybe not everything we thought should be said or done, but REJOICE. The good news has been proclaimed!

PRAY FOR: NEW CALEDONIA

JUNE 3
2 Kings 15, 16; Philippians 2

Our word for today is **GOD EXALTED HIM**.

*...**God exalted him** to the highest place and gave him the name that is above every name* (Philippians 2:9).

It's important not to let society define your success. The only success that matters occurs when God exalts a person. There is no one God has exalted higher than Jesus Christ. If you are feeling snubbed or unappreciated, remember the most highly exalted of God was hung on a cross...for you.

PRAY FOR: NEW ZEALAND

JUNE 4
2 Kings 17, 18; Philippians 3

Our word for today is **SUCCESSFUL.**

*And the LORD was with him; he was **successful** in whatever he undertook...* (2 Kings 18:7).

In this verse, success is predicated with "the Lord was with him." Success is temporary, unless we are walking with the Lord. When we walk with Him, our success grows bigger, step after step.

PRAY FOR: NICARAGUA

JUNE 5
2 Kings 19, 20; Philippians 4

Our word for today is **HEAVEN AND EARTH.**

*"...you alone are God over all the kingdoms of the earth. You have made **heaven and earth**"* (2 Kings 19:15).

How great is our God! He made the heaven and the earth. He created the smallest molecule. He cried at the tomb of Lazarus and rejoiced at a wedding. His understanding and wisdom runs the very fabric of our lives.

PRAY FOR: NIGER

JUNE 6
2 Kings 21, 22, 23; Colossians 1, 2

Our word for today is **SUPREMACY**.

*And he is the head of the body... so that in everything he might have the **supremacy*** (Colossians 1:18).

As a member of the Body of Christ, you are under the leadership of Jesus—He is the Head. You cooperate with the other members of the Body and function as He would function here on earth. He is supreme, and we work to accomplish things for His Kingdom.

PRAY FOR: NIGERIA

JUNE 7
2 Kings 24, 25; Colossians 3

Our word for today is **WORD OF CHRIST**.

*Let the **word of Christ** dwell in you richly... with thankfulness in your hearts to God* (Colossians 3:16, ESV).

The Word of Christ can eternally change things. When we speak what God says, we must believe that it is forever. His Word is not a temporary thing—it's eternal! It's powerful, and we must continue to speak it and believe in its longevity.

PRAY FOR: NIUE

JUNE 8

1 Chronicles 1, 2; Colossians 4

Our word for today is **GRACE.**

*Let your conversation be always full of **grace**, seasoned with salt, so that you may know how to answer everyone* (Colossians 4:6).

What you say is very important. You're going to have to "talk faith," if you expect to "walk faith." Ask God today to give you the words for every conversation, to give you the grace to say exactly what people need to hear!

PRAY FOR: NORTHERN MARIANA ISLANDS

JUNE 9

1 Chronicles 3, 4; 1 Thessalonians 1

Our word for today is **BLESS ME.**

*"... **bless me** and enlarge my territory! Let your hand be with me, and keep me from harm..."* (1 Chronicles 4:10).

Prepare to receive God's blessings in every area of your life. You can prepare by praying, tithing, witnessing, and reading the Word. Believe with faith that He will bless you, and you will receive!

PRAY FOR: NORWAY

JUNE 10
1 Chronicles 5, 6; 1 Thessalonians 2

Our word for today is **BELIEVE.**

*...you received the word of God...which is indeed at work in you who **believe*** (1 Thessalonians 2:13).

When you don't see the thing you've asked and prayed for, do you quit believing? No! There are times when it seems that you wait and wait and wait, but don't cash in on your faith! God is faithful, and when you believe, He is at work!

PRAY FOR: OMAN

JUNE 11
1 Chronicles 7, 8; 1 Thessalonians 3

Our word for today is **INCREASE.**

May the LORD *make your love **increase** and overflow for each other...* (1 Thessalonians 3:12).

God is always moving forward, increasing, enlarging, expanding the universe. Sin is always decreasing, collapsing, dying. When you invite Jesus Christ into your life, you invite increase! Life only gets better and bigger with Him in it.

PRAY FOR: PAKISTAN

JUNE 12
1 Chronicles 9, 10; 1 Thessalonians 4

Our word for today is **AMBITION.**

*...make it your **ambition** to lead a quiet life: You should mind your own business and work with your hands...* (1 Thessalonians 4:11).

Godly ambition takes us places we never expected to go. It can take you to foreign countries or your neighbor's backyard. Selfish ambition isn't quiet or peaceful. It forces its way into places it should never be going.

PRAY FOR: PALAU

JUNE 13
1 Chronicles 11, 12, 13; 1 Thessalonians 5; 2 Thessalonians 1

Our word for today is **MORE POWERFUL.**

*And David became more and **more powerful**, because the LORD Almighty was with him* (1 Chronicles 11:9).

God is omnipotent. Nothing is too difficult for God to do, for He is all powerful. And as a child of God, He extends His power to you and gives you the strength in His name to overcome any obstacle.

PRAY FOR: PALESTINIAN TERRITORIES

JUNE 14
1 Chronicles 14, 15; 2 Thessalonians 2

Our word for today is **SAVED**.

*…God chose you as firstfruits to be **saved** through the sanctifying work of the Spirit…* (2 Thessalonians 2:13).

Have you ever heard the term, "save the best for last"? God plucked us out to be put aside and is saving us for Himself. We are His reward! Isn't it amazing that we are of such value that He considers us the best fruit of all the mighty works He has done?

PRAY FOR: PANAMA

JUNE 15
1 Chronicles 16, 17; 2 Thessalonians 3

Our word for today is **GREAT PROMISES**.

*"…you have done this great thing and made known all these **great promises**"* (1 Chronicles 17:19).

God has made great promises to us in His Word and we can count on those promises. However, when we make a promise to God, He expects us to keep our promises, too. God holds you accountable for the commitments you make.

PRAY FOR: PAPUA NEW GUINEA

JUNE 16
1 Chronicles 18, 19; 1 Timothy 1

Our word for today is **LOVE**.

*The goal of this command is **love**, which comes from a pure heart and a good conscience and a sincere faith* (1 Timothy 1:5).

The notion of love is far reaching and often misunderstood. Many of the examples of love that we see around us are selfish and limited. However, with God in our lives, we can extend a love that comes from a pure heart and a good conscience. He cleanses us and makes us holy, givers and receivers of His love.

PRAY FOR: PARAGUAY

JUNE 17
1 Chronicles 20, 21; 1 Timothy 2

Our word for today is **MEDIATOR**.

*For there is one God and one **mediator** between God and mankind, the man Christ Jesus* (1 Timothy 2:5).

Job lamented and longed for someone to mediate between himself and God. We are so blessed to be part of the generation that has the Mediator, Christ! He stands between us and God's wrath. Because of Him, we only know the goodness and mercy of God.

PRAY FOR: PERU

JUNE 18
1 Chronicles 22, 23; 1 Timothy 3

Our word for today is **SPLENDOR.**

*"...the house...for the LORD should be of great magnificence and fame and **splendor** in the sight of all the nations..."* (1 Chronicles 22:5).

Consider the mighty mountains the Lord has created. Think of the deep oceans with their sandy beaches and turquoise waters. Dream of green forests filled with colorful creatures. Imagine sprawling palaces, with streets of gold. Now consider that the splendor of the Lord goes beyond anything you can imagine! His beauty is breathtaking and awe-inspiring!

PRAY FOR: PHILIPPINES

JUNE 19
1 Chronicles 24, 25; 1 Timothy 4

Our word for today is **VALUE.**

*For physical training is of some value, but godliness has **value** for all things, holding promise...* (1 Timothy 4:8).

God always has light in darkness. When we look to God for our value, we bring that value to all areas of our life! We can be an extension of God's light in the darkness to others.

PRAY FOR: PITCAIRN ISLAND

JUNE 20
1 Chronicles 26, 27, 28; 1 Timothy 5, 6

Our word for today is **THE GOOD FIGHT.**

*Fight **the good fight** of the faith. Take hold of the eternal life to which you were called...* (1 Timothy 6:12).

Our senses will always encourage us to take a one-sided, distorted view of reality, prompting us to make rash decisions which we later regret. Faith fights against this mindset, always telling us to proceed calmly.

PRAY FOR: POLAND

JUNE 21
1 Chronicles 29; 2 Chronicles 1; 2 Timothy 1

Our word for today is **HONOR.**

*Wealth and **honor** come from you; you are the ruler of all things...* (1 Chronicles 29:12).

Wealth and honor come from the Lord. When we seek these things in materialistic ways and trust in the temporary things of this world, we miss out on what God, the Ruler of all things, offers us.

PRAY FOR: PORTUGAL

JUNE 22
2 Chronicles 2, 3; 2 Timothy 2

Our word for today is **REIGN WITH HIM.**

*if we endure, we will also **reign with him**…* (2 Timothy 2:12).

The love of Christ for His Bride is so pure and generous that He made a way for us to reign with Him. His desire was not to have a subordinate to rule over, but rather a sharer in His great inheritance. This is a love that goes deeper than any before or after it.

PRAY FOR: PUERTO RICO

JUNE 23
2 Chronicles 4, 5; 2 Timothy 3

Our word for today is **GLORY.**

*and the priests could not perform their service because of the cloud, for the **glory** of the LORD filled the temple of God* (2 Chronicles 5:14).

The glory of God, so powerful and inspiring, meant Moses was only able to look at the back of God while He passed by him. God's glory literally caused the countenance on Moses' face to be so bright that the people of Israel could not look upon him! Yet we know, in time, we shall see Jesus face to face. We are truly blessed.

PRAY FOR: QATAR

JUNE 24
2 Chronicles 6, 7; 2 Timothy 4

Our word for today is **MY NAME.**

*"... I have chosen Jerusalem for **my Name** to be there, and I have chosen David to rule my people Israel"* (2 Chronicles 6:6).

There is great authority in a name. Your last name tells those around you who birthed you, raised you and launched you into life. The name of Jesus can cast out demons, cast out fear, heal the sick and save the lost.

PRAY FOR: REUNION ISLAND

JUNE 25
2 Chronicles 8, 9; Titus 1

Our word for today is **LIGHT.**

*... he has brought to **light** through the preaching entrusted to me by the command of God our Savior* (Titus 1:3).

You may think that you are one small individual engulfed in a world full of degradation and sin, but remember, your light is always greater than darkness, and God is calling you to penetrate the darkness of your generation.

PRAY FOR: ROMANIA

JUNE 26
2 Chronicles 10, 11; Titus 2

Our word for today is **SALVATION HAS APPEARED.**

*For the grace of God that brings **salvation has appeared** to all men* (Titus 2:11, MEV).

There is something about the phrasing "has appeared" that brings to mind the phrase, "at the last minute." It's almost as if God is telling us, "just when you need it, salvation is given to you."

PRAY FOR: RUSSIAN FEDERATION

JUNE 27
2 Chronicles 12, 13, 14; Titus 3; Philemon

Our word for today is **VICTORIOUS.**

*. . . the people of Judah were **victorious** because they relied on the LORD . . .* (2 Chronicles 13:18).

Jesus is our victory! Jehovah-Nissi, one of the names of the Lord in the Old Testament, reassures us that God is a God who goes before us and brings us to victory when we rely on Him!

PRAY FOR: RWANDA

JUNE 28
2 Chronicles 15, 16; Hebrews 1

Our word for today is **WILL INHERIT**.

*Are not all angels ministering spirits sent to serve those who **will inherit** salvation?* (Hebrews 1:14).

It's important to never lose sight of everything you will inherit. When the road seems long and times are trying, remember... there is an inheritance waiting for you at the end of this season. Salvation is only the deposit of an inheritance that brings so much joy and victory.

PRAY FOR: SAINT KITTS AND NEVIS

JUNE 29
2 Chronicles 17, 18; Hebrews 2

Our word for today is **THRONE**.

*"... I saw the L*ORD* sitting on his **throne** with all the multitudes of heaven standing on his right and on his left"* (2 Chronicles 18:18).

Be at rest, Jesus is on the throne. He is your most trusted Friend, your closest Ally. And He rules all things! Be at peace. He is in charge and His rule will prevail.

PRAY FOR: SAINT LUCIA

JUNE 30
2 Chronicles 19, 20; Hebrews 3

Our word for today is **ENCOURAGE.**

*But **encourage** one another daily, as long as it is called "Today"*... (Hebrews 3:13).

The command to encourage one another is one of the truly remarkable aspects of Christianity. Don't hesitate to give your fellow believers words of encouragement every day. We all need the refreshing that comes from a timely spoken encouragement!

PRAY FOR: SAINT VINCENT AND THE GRENADINES

JULY 1
2 Chronicles 21, 22; Hebrews 4

Our word for today is **SABBATH-REST.**

*There remains, then, a **Sabbath-rest** for the people of God* (Hebrews 4:9).

Did you know that Jewish people start their days at 6 p.m. in the evening? This means they begin their day with a meal and then rest. When they get up to work, their day is already half over! That shows us the significance God places upon rest, His desire is for you to rest and not live in constant stress.

PRAY FOR: SAMOA

JULY 2
2 Chronicles 23, 24; Hebrews 5

Our word for today is **COVENANT.**

*Jehoiada then made a **covenant** that he, the people and the king would be the LORD's people* (2 Chronicles 23:16).

Covenant is such an old-fashioned word and yet the modern-day term, contract, doesn't seem to hold the same significance. It's as if the importance of a deep, long-lasting covenant is lost in this time of quick business deals and even quicker marriages! Let us purpose together to honor the many covenants we have in our lives.

PRAY FOR: SAN MARINO

JULY 3
2 Chronicles 25, 26; Hebrews 6

Our word for today is **FEAR OF GOD.**

*…Zechariah…instructed him [Uzziah] in the **fear of God**. As long as he sought the LORD, God gave him success* (2 Chronicles 26:5).

There are times when children fear their parents and it is a good thing! Fear of consequences, fear of disappointing and fear of hurting our parents can sometimes drive children to the correct action. It's the same with God our Father. While we never need to fear His wrath, it is good to have the same respect toward Him that we carried for our parents.

PRAY FOR: SAO TOME AND PRINCIPE

JULY 4
2 Chronicles 27, 28, 29; Hebrews 7, 8

Our word for today is **BETTER COVENANT.**

*Because of this oath, Jesus has become the guarantor of a **better covenant** (Hebrews 7:22).*

At Mount Sinai, God made a covenant with the children of Israel. This covenant carried the burden of many requirements and consequences. Praise God that in His wisdom, love and mercy, He made a much better covenant in Jesus. A covenant that only has one requirement, believe.

PRAY FOR: SAUDI ARABIA

JULY 5
2 Chronicles 30, 31; Hebrews 9

Our word for today is **RANSOM.**

*…Christ is the mediator of a new covenant… he has died as a **ransom** to set them free…(Hebrews 9:15).*

Jesus Christ abolished the sin that separated you and God. The penalty for your sin has been satisfied and you have life instead of death! Christ is the Mediator, and He paid the ransom for our freedom.

PRAY FOR: SENEGAL

JULY 6
2 Chronicles 32, 33; Hebrews 10

Our word for today is **FAVOR**.

... he sought the favor of the LORD his God and humbled himself greatly before the God of his ancestors (2 Chronicles 33:12).

Favor is a supernatural, unexplainable force of the goodness of God that covers not just the big, but also the small details of your life. You can never win God's love, but you can expect His favor. Favor can lift you beyond normal circumstances and take you further than anything you can do in your own strength!

PRAY FOR: SERBIA

JULY 7
2 Chronicles 34, 35; Hebrews 11

Our word for today is **THROUGH FAITH**.

... through faith conquered kingdoms, administered justice, and gained what was promised... (Hebrews 11:33).

Faith is dynamic! It changes things and makes things happen. It is through our faith that Jesus shows up in our lives. Faith pleases God and brings results, so we should always remember to pursue faith in our lives.

PRAY FOR: SEYCHELLES

JULY 8
2 Chronicles 36; Ezra 1; Hebrews 12

Our word for today is **APPOINTED.**

*... "The LORD ... has **appointed** me to build a temple for him at Jerusalem in Judah ..."* (2 Chronicles 36:23).

Jesus said signs would follow them that believe. He appoints us to flow in the gifts of the Spirit, and you can grow in your gifts. The most important thing to remember is that gifts come out of your relationship with God. You are appointed to do great work for His Kingdom.

PRAY FOR: SIERRA LEONE

JULY 9
Ezra 2, 3; Hebrews 13

Our word for today is **SHOUT OF PRAISE.**

*... all the people gave a great **shout of praise** to the LORD ...* (Ezra 3:11).

Clap your hands and shout because Jesus, the Anointed of God, has won the battle and will subdue all nations under His feet. Jesus won the battle so you can live in victory—you are a winner and that's great cause for shouts of praise!

PRAY FOR: SINGAPORE

JULY 10
Ezra 4, 5; James 1

Our word for today is **TRUTH.**

*He chose to give us birth through the word of **truth**...* (James 1:18).

God is Truth. God cannot lie, and He is true to all that He says. Reality conforms to God's Word, for God's Word is what created reality when He spoke the world into existence. We can trust in the truth of His Word.

PRAY FOR: SLOVAKIA (SLOVAK REPUBLIC)

JULY 11
Ezra 6, 7, 8; James 2, 3

Our word for today is **JOY.**

*Then the people of Israel... celebrated the dedication of the house of God with **joy*** (Ezra 6:16).

There is reason for celebration and joy because we live in God's presence—both now and for eternity. A life with Christ means a life of joy because of the identity we find in Him.

PRAY FOR: SLOVENIA

JULY 12
Ezra 9, 10; James 4

Our word for today is **HUMBLE YOURSELVES.**

Humble yourselves before the Lord, and he will lift you up (James 4:10).

Meekness means self-discipline and humility in your spirit which has to do with your relationship to God. And when that comes forth, it produces a harvest.

PRAY FOR: SOLOMON ISLANDS

JULY 13
Nehemiah 1, 2; James 5

Our word for today is **BE PATIENT.**

. . . be patient and stand firm, because the Lord's coming is near (James 5:8).

When you're going through something difficult, patience can be difficult to find. Things are not always instantaneous. I've had to stand on Scripture for a long time before God brought things to pass. But He is faithful and always comes through.

PRAY FOR: SOMALIA

JULY 14
Nehemiah 3, 4; 1 Peter 1

Our word for today is **REMEMBER.**

*"... Don't be afraid of them. **Remember** the LORD, who is great and awesome..."* (Nehemiah 4:14).

Memory is an amazing and sometimes unreliable gift. The enemy so often wants you to remember the bad things that have happened to you, the broken relationships, the lost opportunities and the disappointments. However, God wants you to remember Him! Remember what He can do and don't let the past stop your future from being all that He's promised!

PRAY FOR: SOUTH AFRICA

JULY 15
Nehemiah 5, 6; 1 Peter 2

Our word for today is **CHOSEN PEOPLE.**

*...you are a **chosen people**, a royal priesthood... God's special possession...* (1 Peter 2:9).

God wants each of us to be a king: To reign in life as God's chosen people, take control of your circumstances, seek God's direction, and learn how to make right, "royal" choices.

PRAY FOR: SOUTH SUDAN

JULY 16
Nehemiah 7, 8; 1 Peter 3

Our word for today is **SACRED.**

*"... This is a **sacred** day before our LORD. Don't be dejected and sad, for the joy of the LORD is your strength!"* (Nehemiah 8:10, NLT).

If we focus on the world and life's struggles, there is reason to feel dejected and sad. But, our God is mighty and strong, and He has overcome the world! When we choose to keep our focus on Him, we have made the day sacred and we can't help but be filled with joy. His joy is truly our strength!

PRAY FOR: SPAIN

JULY 17
Nehemiah 9, 10; 1 Peter 4

Our word for today is **GIVE LIFE.**

*"... You **give life** to everything, and the multitudes of heaven worship you"* (Nehemiah 9:6).

Take a moment to look around you and see the life that God gives ... it's all around you ... in the trees, the green grass, flowers, blue sky, birds. What about the incredible process of growth and renewal that He has given you in your walk with Him? God is life, and He gives life. Let us join the multitudes of heaven in worshipping Him for the life that He gives every day.

PRAY FOR: SRI LANKA

JULY 18
Nehemiah 11, 12, 13; 1 Peter 5; 2 Peter 1

Our word for today is **GLORY**.

*And when the Chief Shepherd appears, you will receive the crown of **glory** that will never fade away* (1 Peter 5:4).

One definition of glory is magnificence and beauty. What could be more beautiful than the gift of His presence? Whenever Jesus is present there is always great glory, beauty and magnificence to be seen.

PRAY FOR: SUDAN

JULY 19
Esther 1, 2; 2 Peter 2

Our word for today is **GODLY PEOPLE**.

*... the LORD knows how to rescue **godly people** from their trials...* (2 Peter 2:9, NLT).

Even godly people have trials and difficult circumstances in life. Godliness is not defined as a lack of trouble or difficulty. The difference between the godly and ungodly is that the godly know the One Who provides a way of escape during temptation, a place of refuge when attacked by the enemies of fear and doubt, and hope for a better future. Trust Him! He will rescue you from your trials.

PRAY FOR: SURINAME

JULY 20
Esther 3, 4; 2 Peter 3

Our word for today is **TIME**.

*"... who knows but that you have come to your royal position for such a **time** as this?"* (Esther 4:14).

You were created for "such a time as this!" Although you may think that you cannot make a significant difference in the world around you, God has His hand upon you in a supernatural way. He wants to use you in His providence during this time on the earth.

PRAY FOR: SWAZILAND

JULY 21
Esther 5, 6; 1 John 1

Our word for today is **WALK IN THE LIGHT**.

*But if we **walk in the light**, as he is in the light, we have fellowship with one another...* (1 John 1:7).

Fellowship within the Body of Christ will build you up spiritually. Being surrounded by other believers will bring fresh revelation and light to your life. When you have others to hold you accountable, you walk in the light as a team.

PRAY FOR: SWEDEN

JULY 22
Esther 7, 8; 1 John 2

Our word for today is **ADVOCATE.**

*... we have an **advocate** with the Father—Jesus Christ, the Righteous One* (1 John 2:1).

You are the righteousness of God in Christ Jesus. God traded your sin for Christ's righteousness, and He advocates for you. He goes before you and behind you to protect you as a child of God!

PRAY FOR: SWITZERLAND

JULY 23
Esther 9, 10; 1 John 3

Our word for today is **CELEBRATION.**

*... their sorrow was turned into joy and their mourning into a day of **celebration**...* (Esther 9:22).

It is amazing how something so awful, like a death or loss, can be a reason for celebration. In the case of Christ, His death is cause for great celebration. His death on the cross was the final sacrifice for sin, the finished work of redemption, and the last effort ever needed for your salvation.

PRAY FOR: SYRIA, SYRIAN ARAB REPUBLIC

JULY 24
Job 1, 2; 1 John 4

Our word for today is **GREATER.**

*You... have overcome them, because the one who is in you is **greater** than the one who is in the world* (1 John 4:4).

When you trust Jesus as your Savior and Lord, you become a member of the greater society. You now have the greatest of all good things living inside of you! The same power that resurrected Christ from the dead lives in you! (See Romans 8:11.) He is greater than any sickness, addiction, disease, or fear.

PRAY FOR: TAIWAN

JULY 25
Job 3, 4, 5; 1 John 5; 2 John

Our word for today is **WALK IN LOVE.**

*...walk in obedience to his commands... his command is that you **walk in love*** (2 John 6).

If we are not cautious, we can fall out of love with people. Often people hurt us, but if we stay in the Word and keep full of the Holy Spirit, then we will love people as we're called to!

PRAY FOR: TAJIKISTAN

JULY 26
Job 6, 7; 3 John

Our word for today is **ATTENTION.**

*"What is mankind that you make so much of them, that you give them so much **attention**"* (Job 7:17).

God has placed immense value and attention on man. He created man in His image and gave man the ultimate expression of value when Jesus died on the cross for us. Join me in humbly thanking Him for the value that He has placed on our lives.

PRAY FOR: TANZANIA, OFFICIALLY THE UNITED REPUBLIC OF TANZANIA

JULY 27
Job 8, 9; Jude

Our word for today is **HOLY SPIRIT.**

*But you, dear friends, by building yourselves up in your most holy faith and praying in the **Holy Spirit*** (Jude 1:20).

The Holy Spirit wants to spend time with us. He is here to comfort, teach, lead, and guide us into God's perfect will each day. Pray in the Holy Spirit, encourage your soul, and build up your "most holy faith."

PRAY FOR: THAILAND

JULY 28
Job 10, 11; Revelation 1

Our word for today is **KINDNESS.**

*You gave me life and showed me **kindness**, and in your providence watched over my spirit* (Job 10:12).

Job had such an amazing revelation of Jesus. God has a way of revealing His love and kindness to us, and Job was able to recognize and acknowledge it in his life, despite the hardships he endured.

PRAY FOR: TIBET

JULY 29
Job 12, 13; Revelation 2

Our word for today is **WISDOM AND POWER.**

*"To God belong **wisdom and power**; counsel and understanding are his"* (Job 12:13).

God is omniscient. He is wise and knows all things. He has perfect wisdom and power and can devise perfect plans and use perfect ways to accomplish them. Know that these traits belong to Him as your perfect Father.

PRAY FOR: TIMOR-LESTE (EAST TIMOR)

JULY 30
Job 14, 15; Revelation 3

Our word for today is **OVERCOMES.**

*"He who **overcomes** shall be clothed in white... I will not blot out his name from the Book of Life..."* (Revelation 3:5, NKJV).

When we allow fear to control us, we hesitate to take first steps in what God calls us to do. When we put our faith in God's promises, He empowers us to overcome big obstacles and step forth to do big things for His kingdom.

PRAY FOR: TOGO

JULY 31
Job 16, 17; Revelation 4

Our word for today is **INTERCESSOR.**

*My **intercessor** is my friend as my eyes pour out tears to God... as one pleads for a friend* (Job 16:20-21).

Intercession causes others to be victorious! Moses was a great intercessor on behalf of the Israelites, and as believers we, too, are called to intercede. Rather than whining about how tough life's battles are, we should be winning life's battles according to God's wisdom.

PRAY FOR: TOKELAU

AUGUST 1
Job 18, 19, 20; Revelation 5, 6

Our word for today is **WORTHY IS THE LAMB.**

"... Worthy is the Lamb, who was slain, to receive power and... honor and glory and praise!" (Revelation 5:12).

Jehovah-Jireh means "the God Who sees ahead and provides." "Jireh" came about as a revelation on Mt. Moriah when God said that He would provide a lamb. Jesus offered Himself as the Lamb for the sins of the world. Worthy is the Lamb because the Lamb is Jesus, who gave Himself for the world.

PRAY FOR: TONGA

AUGUST 2
Job 21, 22; Revelation 7

Our word for today is **PROSPERITY.**

*They spend their years in **prosperity** and go down to the grave in peace* (Job 21:13).

Prosperity in the Lord doesn't necessarily mean monetary wealth. The wisdom of God will show you how to prosper. Get God's wisdom into your life and you won't fail. Prosperity is the wealth and richness of Christ in your life.

PRAY FOR: TRINIDAD AND TOBAGO

AUGUST 3
Job 23, 24; Revelation 8

Our word for today is **INCENSE**.

The smoke of the incense, together with the prayers of God's people, went up before God from the angel's hand (Revelation 8:4).

It is amazing to think that our prayers are like the sweet, intense aroma of incense to God. He loves to hear our prayers, spend time talking with us, and is always ready to listen. Don't hesitate to lift the sweet aroma of your prayers to God today.

PRAY FOR: TUNISIA

AUGUST 4
Job 25, 26; Revelation 9

Our word for today is **DOMINION AND AWE**.

"Dominion and awe belong to God; he establishes order in the heights of heaven" (Job 25:2).

Have you ever just stopped on a clear evening and looked at the stars? There are thousands upon thousands of them that we can see, but even more that we cannot see. It is God who places the stars in their positions, who fashioned the earth's orbit and set in motion all things for your good.

PRAY FOR: TURKEY

AUGUST 5
Job 27, 28; Revelation 10

Our word for today is **WISDOM**.

*"... The fear of the LORD—that is **wisdom**, and to shun evil is understanding"* (Job 28:28).

Fear is usually a negative word for believers, but when it refers to our response to God, it has a different meaning; to respect and honor Him. Choose today to exercise wisdom by honoring God in every area of your life.

PRAY FOR: TURKMENISTAN

AUGUST 6
Job 29, 30; Revelation 11

Our word for today is **GREAT POWER**.

*"... We give thanks to you, Lord God Almighty ... because you have taken your **great power** and have begun to reign"* (Revelation 11:17).

The most common word for God in Revelation is El Shaddai, which means "the God that is more than enough," or "the God that meets our needs in abundance." He has great power now and in the future—this is something to be thankful for! He is more than enough.

PRAY FOR: TURKS AND CAICOS ISLANDS

AUGUST 7
Job 31, 32; Revelation 12

Our word for today is **BREATH.**

*But it is the spirit in a person, the **breath** of the Almighty, that gives them understanding* (Job 32:8).

When God created man from the clay of the earth, it was His breath that gave man life. The same breath that gave Adam life, is the breath that we, as believers, breathe each day. We are alive in our spirit because of the life that was breathed into us through the saving work of Jesus on the cross. Just as Jesus was resurrected from the dead, we, through Him, have been resurrected into new life. Take a long, deep breath today and thank Him for all that He has done for you.

PRAY FOR: TUVALU

AUGUST 8
Job 33, 34, 35; Revelation 13, 14

Our word for today is **NEW SONG.**

*And they sang a **new song** before the throne and before the four living creatures and the elders…* (Revelation 14:3).

When we come to God's throne as believers, committing our lives to Him, we sing a new song. The old is gone, and the new springs forth because of the Spirit dwelling within us. Sing your new song today through your words and actions.

PRAY FOR: UGANDA

AUGUST 9
Job 36, 37; Revelation 15

Our word for today is **CONTENTMENT.**

*If they obey and serve him, they will spend the rest of their... years in **contentment*** (Job 36:11).

Obedience and service require trust in the one that is being obeyed and served. Where is your trust today? Are you trusting in your paycheck, your spouse, your material possessions, or your status in life? Choose to trust in the Lord today. The Father promises that trust in Him will result in contentment.

PRAY FOR: UKRAINE

AUGUST 10
Job 38, 39; Revelation 16

Our word for today is **JUST ARE YOUR JUDGMENTS.**

*"Yes, Lord God Almighty, true and **just are your judgments"*** (Revelation 16:7).

God is just. God sentences the wicked and rewards the righteous according to His Own standards of what is right or wrong. We know that God is just and we can trust His judgments.

PRAY FOR: UNITED ARAB EMIRATES

AUGUST 11
Job 40, 41; Revelation 17

Our word for today is **PURPOSE.**

*For God has put it into their hearts to accomplish his **purpose**...
until God's words are fulfilled* (Revelation 17:17).

There will always be trials, but we should see each one as an opportunity to rise up and achieve God's purpose. We should see these as opportunities for miracles. God puts purpose in your heart, and you are called to fulfill this purpose in your life.

PRAY FOR: UNITED STATES

AUGUST 12
Job 42; Proverbs 1; Revelation 18

Our word for today is **THE LORD BLESSED.**

*The LORD blessed the latter part of Job's life
more than the former part...* (Job 42:12).

Despite the confusion and pain that Job experienced, he never lost his faith. Expect God's blessings. It's very important that you expect God to move in your life and trust that the Lord will bless you, too.

PRAY FOR: URUGUAY

AUGUST 13
Proverbs 2, 3; Revelation 19

Our word for today is **UNDERSTANDING.**

*Blessed are those who find wisdom, those who gain **understanding** (Proverbs 3:13).*

Understanding can settle arguments, calm heated emotions, and be the bridge for differing views or beliefs. Many people today just want to be heard and understood. You are greatly blessed, and equipped for all that life may throw your way, if you find wisdom and gain understanding.

PRAY FOR: UZBEKISTAN

AUGUST 14
Proverbs 4, 5; Revelation 20

Our word for today is **RESURRECTION.**

*Blessed and holy are those who share in the first **resurrection**... (Revelation 20:6).*

Trusting Christ as your Savior means that when He died to sin, you died to sin. And, through His resurrection, you rose again to new life! (See Galatians 2:20) The same power that resurrected Christ from the dead resides in you. (See Romans 8:11.) How blessed we are to share in the resurrection of Jesus Christ!

PRAY FOR: VANUATU

AUGUST 15
Proverbs 6, 7, 8; Revelation 21, 22

Our word for today is **WATER OF LIFE.**

*Let the one who is thirsty come; and let the one who wishes take the free gift of the **water of life*** (Revelation 22:17).

Have you ever been really thirsty? The kind of thirsty where your mouth is dry and your lips are cracked? Sometimes our soul can be this thirsty; wanting refreshment, needing love to quench a feeling of emptiness. Jesus came to quench your soul's thirst. He is the Water of Life that never runs dry and will always satisfy. Take time today to be in His presence, drink from His Word, and enjoy the cleansing, refreshing effects of the Water of Life.

PRAY FOR: VENEZUELA

AUGUST 16
Proverbs 9, 10; Psalm 1

Our word for today is **RIGHTEOUS.**

*For the LORD watches over the way of the **righteous**, but the way of the wicked leads to destruction* (Psalm 1:6).

Jehovah-Tsidkenu, the Lord our righteousness! We have righteousness through Jesus, and there is reason to be thankful because He watches over us.

PRAY FOR: VIETNAM

AUGUST 17
Proverbs 11, 12; Psalm 2

Our word for today is **REFUGE IN HIM.**

Kiss his son, or he will be angry... Blessed are all who take refuge in him (Psalm 2:12).

When David was running from Saul, he sought refuge in many places. He hid in caves, was protected by priests, and even lived among the enemies of Israel. No matter where he was located physically, David always took refuge in his heart, mind and soul in the Lord. No matter where you may be physically located, take refuge in God today. You are blessed when you find your refuge in Him.

PRAY FOR: VIRGIN ISLANDS (BRITISH)

AUGUST 18
Proverbs 13, 14; Psalm 3

Our word for today is **FRUIT.**

From the fruit of their lips people enjoy good things, but the unfaithful have an appetite for violence (Proverbs 13:2).

Remember that it is out of your heart that you bring forth fruit; out of the abundance of the heart the mouth speaks. When we are fruitful, our words reflect our spiritual growth.

PRAY FOR: VIRGIN ISLANDS (UNITED STATES)

AUGUST 19
Proverbs 15, 16; Psalm 4

Our word for today is **SLEEP IN PEACE.**

In peace I will lie down and sleep, for you alone, LORD, make me dwell in safety (Psalm 4:8).

So many people struggle with getting a full night's sleep. Not David. Even while being chased and hunted by Saul, David slept peacefully, for he knew that it was the Lord that sustained him each day. Trust in God to sustain you. He will make you sleep in peace and dwell in safety, giving you security and rest in the storms of life!

PRAY FOR: WALLIS AND FUTUNA ISLANDS

AUGUST 20
Proverbs 17, 18; Psalm 5

Our word for today is **FAVOR.**

Surely, LORD, you bless the righteous; you surround them with your favor as with a shield (Psalm 5:12).

God surrounds the righteous with favor like a shield. And, not just when we are in a battle... at all times! When you go to the doctor, when you shop in a store, at your job, at home, in your relationships... in every area of life you are surrounded with favor like a shield. Expect it, and believe it! Recognize and thank Him for the shield of favor that He surrounds you with each day!

PRAY FOR: WESTERN SAHARA

AUGUST 21
Proverbs 19, 20; Psalm 6

Our word for today is **RESTS.**

*The fear of the LORD leads to life; then one **rests** content, untouched by trouble* (Proverbs 19:23).

Rest is such a powerful word in the Kingdom. Rest indicates a cease from all dead works like self-righteousness, strife, and worry. Trust always accompanies rest. The one who rests in the Lord has chosen to honor the Lord by trusting Him and His promises. Believer, rest today! Know that God understands the challenges that you are facing, the decisions that you need to make, and the potential troubles that might come your way. Trust in Him and rest; all will be well!

PRAY FOR: YEMEN

AUGUST 22
Proverbs 21, 22, 23; Psalm 7, 8

Our word for today is **LEAD TO PROFIT.**

*The plans of the diligent **lead to profit** as surely as haste leads to poverty* (Proverbs 21:5).

Be diligent in whatever you do. God expects us all to be good, hard workers. Laziness will keep you from reaching your full potential. But purposeful work leads to profit across several areas of your life.

PRAY FOR: ZAMBIA

AUGUST 23
Proverbs 24, 25; Psalm 9

Our word for today is **THRONE**.

*For You have maintained my right and my cause; You sat on the **throne** judging in righteousness* (Psalm 9:4, NKJV).

Know that the One who sits on the throne sees your cause, whatever it may be today, and will rightly execute judgement on your behalf.

PRAY FOR: ZIMBABWE

AUGUST 24
Proverbs 26, 27; Psalm 10

Our word for today is **PRAISE**.

*Let someone else **praise** you, and not your own mouth; an outsider, and not your own lips* (Proverbs 27:2).

With the glitter and glamour of this world, it is easy to think that we need to promote ourselves to be seen. Not so in the Kingdom. God sees you. He sees your heart, and knows your deeds. It takes great courage and humility to remain faithful to God even when no one acknowledges or even understands your actions, or when you receive no praise from others. The Lord sees you...stay the course!

PRAY FOR THE ETHNIC GROUP: ACHOLI

AUGUST 25
Proverbs 28, 29; Psalm 11

Our word for today is **SEE HIS FACE.**

For the LORD is righteous, he loves justice; the upright will see his face (Psalm 11:7).

Have you ever felt like the Lord was smiling at you? Like you could see His face? He is smiling at you right now. He loves you, and wants nothing more than for you to know His love and how He delights in you.

PRAY FOR THE ETHNIC GROUP: AKAN

AUGUST 26
Proverbs 30, 31; Psalm 12

Our word for today is **SON.**

"… Who has established all the ends of the earth? What is his name, and what is the name of his son? Surely you know!" (Proverbs 30:4).

There is none more mighty and powerful than God, His Son, and the Holy Spirit. And, as a believer, you have the Trinity available to you every day! Thank the Father, Son, and Spirit for their presence in your life today!

PRAY FOR THE ETHNIC GROUP: ALBANIANS

AUGUST 27
Ecclesiastes 1, 2; Psalm 13

Our word for today is **PLEASES.**

*To the person who **pleases** him, God gives wisdom, knowledge and happiness...* (Ecclesiastes 2:26).

As believers, we all want to please God. And, we know from Hebrews that it is impossible to please God without faith. What is faith but trusting and believing that what God has promised, He will fulfill. It is amazing that the very thing that pleases Him is what gives us wisdom, knowledge and happiness.

PRAY FOR THE ETHNIC GROUP: AFAR

AUGUST 28
Ecclesiastes 3,4; Psalm 14

Our word for today is **SEEK.**

*The LORD looks down from heaven on all mankind to see if there are any who understand, any who **seek** God* (Psalm 14:2).

A lot of times we try to figure out the answers ourselves and rely on our intellect. Then, when nothing works, we finally call on God. We shouldn't wait. Our first reaction should be to seek God.

PRAY FOR THE ETHNIC GROUP: AFRIKANERS

AUGUST 29
Ecclesiastes 5, 6, 7; Psalm 15, 16

Our word for today is **COUNSELS ME.**

*I will praise the LORD, who **counsels me**; even at night my heart instructs me* (Psalm 16:7).

What a comfort to know that no matter what demanding situation I am facing, the Lord will always be there to counsel me. He is there to counsel us in the good times and bad. The Lord is available and ready to answer our prayers. Let's join the psalmist and praise Him for His counsel and guidance every day.

PRAY FOR THE ETHNIC GROUP: AMHARA

AUGUST 30
Ecclesiastes 8, 9; Psalm 17

Our word for today is **BRIGHTENS.**

*Who is like the wise... A person's wisdom **brightens** their face and changes its hard appearance* (Ecclesiastes 8:1).

Each of us is given opportunities through God's providence to change our world for the better. When we receive wisdom from God, we can bring light to the darkness of this world. Are you accepting and using these opportunities to be brightened through His wisdom?

PRAY FOR THE ETHNIC GROUP: ARABS

AUGUST 31
Ecclesiastes 10, 11; Psalm 18

Our word for today is **DEEP WATERS.**

He reached down from on high and took hold of me;
*he drew me out of **deep waters** (Psalm 18:16).*

Sometimes the decisions that we make in life seem like swimming in deep waters. When you feel like you've swum out too far or gotten too deep into waters that are unclear and muddy, know that you can call upon Him. Look to Him! He will take hold of you, and draw you out of deep waters. Like a loving parent, the Lord knows the places that are best for you. (Psalm 121:7) He will keep you safe.

PRAY FOR THE ETHNIC GROUP: ARMENIANS

SEPTEMBER 1
Ecclesiastes 12; Song of Songs 1; Psalm 19

Our word for today is **THE GLORY OF GOD.**

*The heavens declare **the glory of God**; the skies*
proclaim the work of his hands (Psalm 19:1).

The glory of God is all around us, but nowhere more apparent than in the sky. By day, we see the majestic clouds and the bright, bold sun. And, by night, we see millions of stars and the moon. Let us praise Him for how He has surrounded us with His glory!

PRAY FOR THE ETHNIC GROUP: ASSAMESE

SEPTEMBER 2
Song of Songs 2, 3; Psalm 20

Our word for today is **BANNER**.

Let him lead me to the banquet hall, and let his ***banner*** *over me be love* (Song of Songs 2:4).

When a banner was used during biblical times it represented the name of a tribe or family. In battle, the banner was shown before the trumpet was blown. How comforting and reassuring to know that the banner over you is His love! You belong to Him, and to His family, which is love! When you fight enemies like fear, doubt, addiction, insecurity and lust... remember that His banner over you is love. And His love never fails! (1 Corinthians 13)

PRAY FOR THE ETHNIC GROUP: ASSYRIANS

SEPTEMBER 3
Song of Songs 4, 5; Psalm 21

Our word for today is **ALTOGETHER BEAUTIFUL**.

You are ***altogether beautiful****, my darling; there is no flaw in you* (Song of Songs 4:7).

When God sees you, He sees the altogether beautiful and wonderful son or daughter of His that you are. He sees one that has been redeemed, forgiven, washed clean and made righteous by Jesus' death and resurrection. You are altogether beautiful in His sight!

PRAY FOR THE ETHNIC GROUP: AZERBAIJANIS

SEPTEMBER 4
Song of Songs 6, 7; Psalm 22

Our word for today is **SATISFIED**.

*The poor will eat and be **satisfied**; those who seek the LORD will praise him...* (Psalm 22:26).

The NIV says the poor, but there are other Bible translations that describe the hungry as the oppressed, the afflicted, the down-and-outers. No matter if you are poor, afflicted, oppressed or just down-and-out, the Lord wants to feed and nourish you!

PRAY FOR THE ETHNIC GROUP: BALOCHIS

SEPTEMBER 5
Song of Songs 8; Isaiah 1, 2; Psalm 23, 24

Our word for today is **SCARLET**.

*"... Though your sins are like **scarlet**, they shall be as white as snow; though they are red as crimson, they shall be like wool"* (Isaiah 1:18).

It takes a great deal of bleach to remove a stain from a white shirt. Even after many tries, sometimes the stain just won't come out. Stronger than bleach or any human effort, the blood shed from Jesus' death, and that covers you and me today, is the solvent that washes our scarlet sins away and makes us white as snow. Clean, fresh, brand-new... you are forgiven!

PRAY FOR THE ETHNIC GROUP: BAMARS

SEPTEMBER 6
Isaiah 3, 4; Psalm 25

Our word for today is **WAYS OF THE LORD.**

*All the **ways of the LORD** are loving and faithful toward those who keep the demands of his covenant* (Psalm 25:10).

God does not lead with an iron fist, nor is He a foreboding force that drives His children to obey. Instead, the ways of the Lord are loving and faithful toward you. Choose to follow Him today. Praise Him for His lovingkindness and faithfulness toward His children!

PRAY FOR THE ETHNIC GROUP: BAMBARA

SEPTEMBER 7
Isaiah 5, 6; Psalm 26

Our word for today is **TEST ME.**

***Test me**, LORD, and try me, examine my heart and my mind; for I have always been mindful of your unfailing love...* (Psalm 26:2-3).

It's when I am mindful of His unfailing love for me, that I can willingly invite the Lord to test me and examine my heart and mind. There is no fear of failure when we are enveloped and consistently mindful of His love. Love never fails! (See 1 Corinthians 13.) Stay mindful of His unfailing love... He will never fail you!

PRAY FOR THE ETHNIC GROUP: BASHKIRS

SEPTEMBER 8
Isaiah 7, 8; Psalm 27

Our word for today is **SIGN**.

> ... the LORD himself will give you a **sign**:
> The virgin will conceive and give birth to a son,
> and will call him Immanuel (Isaiah 7:14).

The birth of Jesus is the sign that we are living under a new covenant; signed and sealed, not validated by the sacrifice of a bull and lamb, but by the final sacrifice—Jesus! No longer do we receive the law from far atop a mountain, but now we have been given the gift of grace through the person of Jesus Christ.

PRAY FOR THE ETHNIC GROUP: BASQUES

SEPTEMBER 9
Isaiah 9, 10; Psalm 28

Our word for today is **REJOICE**.

> You have... increased their joy; they **rejoice** before you
> as people rejoice at the harvest... (Isaiah 9:3).

The rejoicing that goes on at harvest is like a party; the work's done, the benefit has been gathered, and the storehouse is full! Praise God that with Jesus the work has been done, the benefit from His work is ours, and we, and all who receive from His labor, are filled and satisfied now and forever. Rejoice!

PRAY FOR THE ETHNIC GROUP: BELARUSIANS

SEPTEMBER 10
Isaiah 11, 12; Psalm 29

Our word for today is **WORSHIP THE LORD.**

*Ascribe to the LORD the glory due his name; **worship the LORD** in the splendor of his holiness* (Psalm 29:2).

Worship is the acknowledgement that God is God. In worship, you thank God for being Who He is. Should you feel "far" from God's presence, then just start worshipping Him, for the Holy Spirit manifests Himself in your times of praise and worship.

PRAY FOR THE ETHNIC GROUP: BEMBA

SEPTEMBER 11
Isaiah 13, 14; Psalm 30

Our word for today is **REST.**

*The LORD has broken the rod of the wicked... All the lands are at **rest** and at peace; they break into singing* (Isaiah 14:5, 7).

Jesus promises in Matthew 11:28 that He will give us rest. He is our rest! We can take every burden, problem, struggle, and pain to Him and He will give us rest. He is the answer to every question, and the solution to every problem. Take your cares and concerns to Him and receive the rest that He freely gives.

PRAY FOR THE ETHNIC GROUP: BENGALIS

SEPTEMBER 12
Isaiah 15, 16, 17; Psalm 31, 32

Our word for today is **STORED UP.**

*How abundant are the good things that you have **stored up** for those who fear you... who take refuge in you* (Psalm 31:19).

When you choose to trust the Lord with your life, you are taking shelter in the abundance of His house (Psalm 23:6); the place where all good things are stored up. He has peace stored up for you. He has rest stored up for you. He has mercy and grace stored up for you. And, His supply is endless, it will never dry up or fade away. It is always available to you. Ask, and you shall receive!

PRAY FOR THE ETHNIC GROUP: BERBERS

SEPTEMBER 13
Isaiah 18, 19; Psalm 33

Our word for today is **TRUMPET.**

*...when a banner is raised on the mountains, you will see it, and when a **trumpet** sounds, you will hear it* (Isaiah 18:3).

A trumpet is a beautiful instrument. It is used in orchestras, to give the signal for battle, and as a solemn a cappella when honoring those servicemen that have given their life for our country. As believers, we all listen for that last trumpet sound that will signal Jesus' return. The next time that you hear a trumpet sound, remember that He is coming soon.

PRAY FOR THE ETHNIC GROUP: BETI-PAHUIN

SEPTEMBER 14
Isaiah 20, 21; Psalm 34

Our word for today is **EXTOL.**

*I will **extol** the LORD at all times; his praise will always be on my lips* (Psalm 34:1).

Extol doesn't just mean to praise, but to praise enthusiastically. Praise Him! Enthusiastically, praise Him always! He is deserving of our praise for all the remarkable things that He has done.

PRAY FOR THE ETHNIC GROUP: BOSNIAKS

SEPTEMBER 15
Isaiah 22, 23; Psalm 35

Our word for today is **HIS SALVATION.**

*Then my soul will rejoice in the LORD and delight in **his salvation*** (Psalm 35:9).

What have you been saved from today? Was it a near-miss accident, a relationship that might have destroyed everything, or maybe a poor financial decision? Delight in His salvation. He saves not only our souls for all eternity, but He also saves us daily from ordinary circumstances or instances that Satan uses to try to kill, steal, and destroy us. Praise God for His daily salvation!

PRAY FOR THE ETHNIC GROUP: BRAHUI

SEPTEMBER 16
Isaiah 24, 25; Psalm 36

Our word for today is **FAITHFULNESS.**

LORD... *in perfect **faithfulness** you have done wonderful things, things planned long ago* (Isaiah 25:1).

The Lord has a perfect plan for your life, and He is faithful to follow through on His promises. He will give you the spiritual desire to bring that plan into fulfillment, and He will guide you along the way.

PRAY FOR THE ETHNIC GROUP: BRITISH

SEPTEMBER 17
Isaiah 26, 27; Psalm 37

Our word for today is **PEACE.**

*"Or else let them come to me for refuge; let them make **peace** with me, yes, let them make peace with me"* (Isaiah 27:5).

Peace with God is such a good feeling. Knowing that you have been forgiven and that God is not angry with you is an incredible feeling. It is easy to attain... you already have it! Realize that because of the Cross, you have peace with God!

PRAY FOR THE ETHNIC GROUP: BULGARIANS

SEPTEMBER 18
Isaiah 28, 29; Psalm 38

Our word for today is **WAIT FOR YOU.**

LORD, **I wait for you**; *you will answer,* LORD *my God* (Psalm 38:15).

There are things I've prayed over for years and years and I am just now seeing them come to pass. It is so important that we faithfully wait for the Lord; don't give up! This is what the Lord has said to me about this: when you put your hand on heaven, heaven puts its hand on you.

PRAY FOR THE ETHNIC GROUP: CATALANS

SEPTEMBER 19
Isaiah 30, 31, 32; Psalm 39, 40

Our word for today is **SHEILD.**

"... *the* LORD *Almighty will shield Jerusalem; he will* **shield** *it and deliver it, he will 'pass over' it and will rescue it"* (Isaiah 31:5).

The most insignificant of nations, small in size, and surrounded by opposing nations, history has shown and the Bible tells us that Israel is shielded by God. You may be feeling insignificant, small, and surrounded by enemies like fear, doubt, and unbelief. Know today that just as the Lord Almighty has been a shield to Jerusalem, He is a shield to you.

PRAY FOR THE ETHNIC GROUP: CHUVASH

SEPTEMBER 20
Isaiah 33, 34; Psalm 41

Our word for today is **RICH**.

*He will be the sure foundation for your times, a **rich** store of salvation and wisdom and knowledge; the fear of the LORD is the key to this treasure* (Isaiah 33:6).

There is an economy in the Kingdom of God. It's not based on money, material possessions, status, or fame. God's economy and the transactions that take place in His Kingdom have eternal worth; salvation, hope, peace...love. Jesus purchased it all for us. We are the "richest" people on the earth!

PRAY FOR THE ETHNIC GROUP: CIRCASSIANS

SEPTEMBER 21
Isaiah 35, 36; Psalm 42

Our word for today is **STREAMS OF WATER**.

*As the deer pants for **streams of water**, so my soul pants for you, my God* (Psalm 42:1).

This psalmist shows us that when we set our eyes on our Creator instead of our condition, we receive peace, confidence and have the response of praise. The Lord is our living water—sustenance for our souls!

PRAY FOR THE ETHNIC GROUP: CHEWA

SEPTEMBER 22
Isaiah 37, 38; Psalm 43

Our word for today is **KINGDOMS.**

*". . . you alone are God over all the **kingdoms** of the earth. You have made heaven and earth"* (Isaiah 37:16).

There are governmental authorities in every country. There are natural laws that govern space and time, and, spiritual forces that are always pushing for influence in our minds. Is it not reassuring and comforting to know that God alone is Ruler over all kingdoms? Whether it be a physical, natural, or spiritual kingdom, He is Ruler of them all!

PRAY FOR THE ETHNIC GROUP: HAN

SEPTEMBER 23
Isaiah 39, 40; Psalm 44

Our word for today is **GIVE US VICTORY.**

*. . . you **give us victory** over our enemies, you put our adversaries to shame* (Psalm 44:7).

Take time today to thank God for our local and national officials. We know that God gives us victory, so we can confidently intercede on behalf of our leaders so that even in the face of a great challenge, they will boldly declare "In God We Trust!"

PRAY FOR THE ETHNIC GROUP: CORNISH

SEPTEMBER 24
Isaiah 41, 42; Psalm 45

Our word for today is **JUSTICE**.

Your throne, O God, will last for ever and ever; a scepter of justice will be the scepter of your kingdom (Psalm 45:6).

A scepter is an ornamental staff that acts as a symbol of sovereignty. Our God is the sovereign authority in all matters relating to justice. He is the only one that can rightly hold a scepter of justice. His rule is supreme, and none can contend His verdict. Praise Him that He has found those covered by the sacrificial blood of Jesus not guilty!

PRAY FOR THE ETHNIC GROUP: CORSICANS

SEPTEMBER 25
Isaiah 43, 44; Psalm 46

Our word for today is **OFFSPRING**.

*. . . I will pour out my Spirit on your **offspring**, and my blessing on your descendants* (Isaiah 44:3).

This is a promise. The Lord will pour out His Spirit on your offspring, and blessings upon your children's children. Your family is blessed because of your decision to follow Jesus!

PRAY FOR THE ETHNIC GROUP: CROATS

SEPTEMBER 26
Isaiah 45, 46, 47; Psalm 47, 48

Our word for today is **AWESOME LORD.**

For the LORD Most High is awesome, the great King over all the earth (Psalm 47:2).

You are living in the afterglow of the most tremendous battle fought in history. The Son of God defeated Satan at Calvary and the door to salvation was opened to all who would believe on the name of Jesus. He is awesome!

PRAY FOR THE ETHNIC GROUP: CZECHS

SEPTEMBER 27
Isaiah 48, 49; Psalm 49

Our word for today is **BEST.**

"... I am the LORD your God, who teaches you what is best for you, who directs you in the way you should go" (Isaiah 48:17).

Every day is filled with decisions; simple ones like where to park, what to eat, what to wear, and, more difficult ones like what to say when someone is hurting, whom to marry, or what job to take. It is a blessing to have a choice and a privilege to be able to choose. But, if you're wondering what is best, seek Him. He will teach you what is best for you, and direct you in which way you should go. Praise God that He is our faithful Guide and helps us to choose what is best.

PRAY FOR THE ETHNIC GROUP: DANES

SEPTEMBER 28
Isaiah 50, 51; Psalm 50

Our word for today is **LAST FOREVER.**

*"... my salvation will **last forever**, my righteousness will never fail"* (Isaiah 51:6).

We live in a very consumer-oriented world. Many of the items we purchase in life are designed to be replaced, and only last a few years. Even relationships don't last forever; loved ones pass away, friends move to different states. But we know that our salvation from the Lord lasts forever, and that His righteousness never fails. The salvation from the Lord is designed to be eternal; it can never be damaged, used up, or destroyed! We can count on God and what He has done for us.

PRAY FOR THE ETHNIC GROUP: DINKA

SEPTEMBER 29
Isaiah 52, 53; Psalm 51

Our word for today is **CLEANSE.**

***Cleanse** me with hyssop, and I will be clean; wash me, and I will be whiter than snow* (Psalm 51:7).

The cleansing power of Jesus' blood purifies your heart from the inside out. It removes the filth of sin and uncleanness from your daily life, purifying your heart so perfectly that you actually become a temple of God!

PRAY FOR THE ETHNIC GROUP: DUTCH

SEPTEMBER 30
Isaiah 54, 55; Psalm 52

Our word for today is **JOY.**

You will go out in joy and be led forth in peace; the mountains and hills will burst into song before you... (Isaiah 55:12).

Stay close to Him, keep your mind on Him, and His joy will be with you and His peace will guide you every day.

PRAY FOR THE ETHNIC GROUP: ENGLISH

OCTOBER 1
Isaiah 56, 57; Psalm 53

Our word for today is **REFUGE.**

*"... But whoever takes **refuge** in me will inherit the land and possess my holy mountain"* (Isaiah 57:13).

The Bible says that God is your refuge—a place where you can go quietly and be protected from harm. He is your strength, and the best part is, you don't have to look for Him because He's always in your midst—right in your heart.

PRAY FOR THE ETHNIC GROUP: ESTONIANS

OCTOBER 2
Isaiah 58, 59: Psalm 54

Our word for today is **GOD IS MY HELP.**

*Surely **God is my help;** the* LORD *is the one who sustains me* (Psalm 54:4).

We don't have to rely on ourselves or other people to help us out in times of trouble. God is your help! He will pull you out of every dark time and sustain you through any trial you may face.

PRAY FOR THE ETHNIC GROUP: FAROESE

OCTOBER 3
Isaiah 60, 61, 62; Psalm 55, 56

Our word for today is **CROWN.**

*... bestow on them a **crown** of beauty instead of ashes, the oil of joy instead of mourning, and a garment of praise...* (Isaiah 61:3).

God is gifted at using the dark things of our past to reveal His beauty. It's our ugly past that He snatched us out of that now gives us compassion for others that go down the same dark roads we once traveled. It's the sorrow and mourning of a youth lost that serves as a platform for His renewal and restoration. And, that crown that we once wore of brokenness, insecurity, and fear, He has replaced with a crown of beauty. God is so good to us!

PRAY FOR THE ETHNIC GROUP: FINNS

OCTOBER 4
Isaiah 63, 64; Psalm 57

Our word for today is **PRAISE YOU.**

*I will **praise you**, LORD, among the nations; I will sing of you among the peoples* (Psalm 57:9).

Please join with me today: Lord, I praise You! I praise You for being Lord over all the nations and all the peoples of the earth. Let every tongue, tribe, and all people praise You, Father!

PRAY FOR THE ETHNIC GROUP: FRENCH

OCTOBER 5
Isaiah 65, 66; Psalm 58

Our word for today is **RIGHTEOUS.**

"... *Surely the **righteous** still are rewarded; surely there is a God who judges the earth*" (Psalm 58:11).

There isn't always an immediate reward for doing good. Sometimes the reward is delayed. The Lord promises in this verse that the righteous will be rewarded.

PRAY FOR THE ETHNIC GROUP: FRISIANS

OCTOBER 6
Jeremiah 1, 2; Psalm 59

Our word for today is **BORN**.

*"Before I formed you in the womb I knew you, before you were **born** I set you apart..."* (Jeremiah 1:5).

You may not think that others know you, but for sure God does. He knows you. He knew you before you were born. He knew what color your hair would be, whether you would prefer chocolate over vanilla, your weaknesses and your passions. He knows you! And, He gave His Son to you, before you were born, to set you apart and make you His own.

PRAY FOR THE ETHNIC GROUP: FULA

OCTOBER 7
Jeremiah 3, 4; Psalm 60

Our word for today is **GAIN THE VICTORY**.

*With God we will **gain the victory**, and he will trample down our enemies* (Psalm 60:12).

If you plan to live victoriously, remember that it is God's Word that is strategic to your fight. Spend time in His Word and in prayer. Have faith that the Lord paves the way to victory!

PRAY FOR THE ETHNIC GROUP: GA-ADANGBE

OCTOBER 8
Jeremiah 5, 6; Psalm 61

Our word for today is **REST**.

> *"... ask where the good way is, and walk in it, and you will find **rest** for your souls..."* (Jeremiah 6:16).

Although it is no easy thing to rest in the Lord, if you trust God for your victory, you will realize that God's continual presence is sufficient to meet your every challenge. Ask Him to guide you in your walk, and rest will come easily!

PRAY FOR THE ETHNIC GROUP: GAGAUZ

OCTOBER 9
Jeremiah 7, 8; Psalm 62

Our word for today is **COMFORTER**.

> *You who are my **Comforter** in sorrow, my heart is faint within me* (Jeremiah 8:18).

When a person experiences a loss, the grief can seem unbearable. You might ask yourself, will it ever go away; will I ever feel normal again? Jesus said that in this world there would be many sorrows, but to take heart because He has overcome the world (see John 16:33). And, He has given us a Comforter, the Holy Spirit. Take all your troubles, sorrows and grief to the Lord and let Him wrap His comfort around you like a warm blanket. God cares for you, and wants to comfort you in your time of sorrow.

PRAY FOR THE ETHNIC GROUP: GALICIAN

OCTOBER 10
Jeremiah 9, 10, 11; Psalm 63, 64

Our word for today is **BETTER THAN LIFE.**

*Because your love is **better than life**, my lips will glorify you* (Psalm 63:3).

The Father gives us better-than-life love—a love that surpasses space, the laws of nature, or even feeling. It is eternal, transcending time. It is consistent and real. Praise You, Father, that we are loved by You!

PRAY FOR THE ETHNIC GROUP: GANDA

OCTOBER 11
Jeremiah 12, 13; Psalm 65

Our word for today is **ABUNDANCE.**

*You crown the year with your bounty, and your carts overflow with **abundance*** (Psalm 65:11).

Do you believe that the Lord wants you to live a life of abundance? He does! He sent His Son that you might have life, and have it more abundantly (see John 10:10).

PRAY FOR THE ETHNIC GROUP: GERMANS

OCTOBER 12
Jeremiah 14, 15; Psalm 66

Our word for today is **GOOD.**

*... "Surely I will deliver you for a **good** purpose; surely I will make your enemies plead with you..."* (Jeremiah 15:11).

God's goodness is so much bigger and brighter than any wickedness we are exposed to on this earth. Once we have tasted of God's goodness, we see that His purpose for our life and His power to deliver us from darkness is bigger and better than anything we could ever imagine.

PRAY FOR THE ETHNIC GROUP: GREEKS

OCTOBER 13
Jeremiah 16, 17; Psalm 67

Our word for today is **BE GRACIOUS.**

*May God **be gracious** to us and bless us and make his face shine on us* (Psalm 67:1).

Being gracious is a lost characteristic. Many think it is better to "get things done" or move quickly, and forego the time it takes to consider others. God is always gracious to us. He patiently waits and takes time to hear our prayers and see our heart. Thank You, Father, that we can learn how to be gracious to others by the graciousness that You have shown us.

PRAY FOR THE ETHNIC GROUP: GEORGIANS

OCTOBER 14
Jeremiah 18, 19; Psalm 68

Our word for today is **POWER.**

*Summon your **power**, God; show us your strength, our God, as you have done before* (Psalm 68:28).

It's been at my weakest moments that I have seen God's greatest power at work in my life. And by power, I mean dunamis, miracle-working power! We have seen His strength before, and we will see it again.

PRAY FOR THE ETHNIC GROUP: GUARANIS

OCTOBER 15
Jeremiah 20, 21; Psalm 69

Our word for today is **MIGHTY WARRIOR.**

*But the LORD is with me like a **mighty warrior**; so my persecutors will stumble...* (Jeremiah 20:11).

When you stay in the Word, you will see that God is a mighty warrior who fights for you. Your persecutors don't stand a chance against an all-powerful God!

PRAY FOR THE ETHNIC GROUP: GUJARATI

OCTOBER 16
Jeremiah 22, 23; Psalm 70

Our word for today is **REJOICE.**

*...may all who seek you **rejoice** and be glad in you...* (Psalm 70:4).

We have cause to rejoice when we seek the Lord, because He can be found. He doesn't play hide-and-seek or run away when we call His name. He is always available, waiting for us to desire His presence and His Word in our lives. His desire is for us to seek Him. He wants to be found by you!

PRAY FOR THE ETHNIC GROUP: HADIYA

OCTOBER 17
Jeremiah 24, 25, 26; Psalm 71, 72

Our word for today is **HEART.**

*I will give them a **heart** to know me, that I am the LORD. They will be my people...* (Jeremiah 24:7).

One of the many wonderful changes that happen when you receive Christ as your Savior is He gives you a new heart. Suddenly there is an abundance of hope for every troublesome situation, an insatiable hunger to know God and His Word, and burdens that used to weigh you down now feel light. He helps us to see with eyes of faith, with a sense that we belong to Someone greater than ourselves. Praise Him for how He makes all things brand new!

PRAY FOR THE ETHNIC GROUP: HAUSA

OCTOBER 18
Jeremiah 27, 28; Psalm 73

Our word for today is **COUNSEL.**

*You guide me with your **counsel**, and afterward you will take me into glory* (Psalm 73:24).

One of the most comforting things about God is that He does not leave us to our own minds and hearts. Left to our own mind, we might believe a lie. And sometimes our heart betrays us. Praise Him, that we don't have to figure out the answer to life's problems; that we have Him to guide and counsel us each day.

PRAY FOR THE ETHNIC GROUP: HUI

OCTOBER 19
Jeremiah 29, 30; Psalm 74

Our word for today is **TO PROSPER.**

*"For I know the plans I have for you... plans **to prosper** you... plans to give you hope and a future"* (Jeremiah 29:11).

God's past goodness is grounds for confidence and assurance in what lies ahead. God has great plans for goodness in your life, and when we reflect on the good things He has done in the past, we build confidence for the future and the ways in which He brings prosperity.

PRAY FOR THE ETHNIC GROUP: HUNGARIANS

OCTOBER 20
Jeremiah 31, 32; Psalm 75

Our word for today is **NEAR.**

*We praise you, God... for your Name is **near**; people tell of your wonderful deeds* (Psalm 75:1).

If you listen carefully in church, the Name of God is always near. Someone is talking about how He healed their loved one, how He gave their family a financial miracle, and others speak about how He rescued their son or daughter from a life of addiction. God's miracle-working name is always being spoken with gratitude and awe at His wondrous deeds! Thank Him today for always being near.

PRAY FOR THE ETHNIC GROUP: IBIBIO

OCTOBER 21
Jeremiah 33, 34; Psalm 76

Our word for today is **HEAL.**

*"... I will **heal** my people and will let them enjoy abundant peace and security"* (Jeremiah 33:6).

Our Heavenly Father wants us to be whole and well and strong in our bodies, our spirits, our souls. He works healing miracles even to this day. Maybe you have pain, arthritis, a bone missing—God has spare parts in Heaven. He wants to heal you today!

PRAY FOR THE ETHNIC GROUP: ICELANDERS

OCTOBER 22
Jeremiah 35, 36; Psalm 77

Our word for today is **MIRACLES**.

*You are the God who performs **miracles**; you display your power among the peoples* (Psalm 77:14).

Believe this today: God can give you a miracle in your life. Go to God expecting the miraculous! When you take on an attitude of disbelief or doubt, you step away from faith and accept something that isn't biblical. Go to God today with your miracle need and expect to see Him at work in your life!

PRAY FOR THE ETHNIC GROUP: IJAW

OCTOBER 23
Jeremiah 37, 38; Psalm 78

Our word for today is **NEXT GENERATION**.

*. . . tell the **next generation** the praiseworthy deeds of the LORD . . .* (Psalm 78:4).

It's good to ensure that amid the busyness of social media, video games and television, your children hear the life-giving Word of God and all the wonderful things that He has done in your life. Give the next generation the Good News that will stay with them to eternity.

PRAY FOR THE ETHNIC GROUP: IRISH

OCTOBER 24
Jeremiah 39, 40, 41; Psalm 79, 80

Our word for today is **RESCUE.**

*But I will **rescue** you on that day, declares the LORD; you will not be given into the hands of those you fear* (Jeremiah 39:17).

The Lord knows what you are wrestling with. He knows who and what you fear. Fear is unhealthy and can cause you to do things that you would not normally do. Before you give in to that fear, cry out to the Lord. As you read His Word, ask Him for guidance and direction. Tell Him how you are feeling, and what you are afraid of. Trust Him and His Word. He will rescue you!

PRAY FOR THE ETHNIC GROUP: ITALIANS

OCTOBER 25
Jeremiah 42, 43; Psalm 81

Our word for today is **SING FOR JOY.**

***Sing for joy** to God our strength; shout aloud to the God of Jacob!* (Psalm 81:1).

The enemy raises his voice to frighten and intimidate. But, we, the ones strengthened by God, raise our voices to sing for joy and shout aloud for all the great things that God has done for us!

PRAY FOR THE ETHNIC GROUP: JAPANESE

OCTOBER 26
Jeremiah 44, 45; Psalm 82

Our word for today is **NATIONS.**

*Rise up, O God, judge the earth, for all the **nations** are your inheritance* (Psalm 82:8).

Nothing gets past our Lord. He knows the heart of man, and the evil deeds that man can do. He will rise and judge the nations for every evil deed that has been done to mankind. How God loves us all! He will not let the unjust prevail!

PRAY FOR THE ETHNIC GROUP: JAVANESE

OCTOBER 27
Jeremiah 46, 47; Psalm 83

Our word for today is **MOST HIGH.**

*… you alone are the **Most High** over all the earth* (Psalm 83:18).

The Creator of all is the Most High over all! Everything is subject to His reign! Every circumstance or situation; every dimension of time, space, and ability; and all worldly authorities are subject to His reign.

PRAY FOR THE ETHNIC GROUP: JEWS

OCTOBER 28
Jeremiah 48, 49; Psalm 84

Our word for today is **PROTECT.**

*"But I will **protect** the orphans who remain among you. Your widows, too, can depend on me for help"* (Jeremiah 49:11, NLT).

Are you feeling displaced, cut-off, like you're not sure that you belong anywhere? We all have moments when we struggle with these feelings. Know that the Lord, the God that protects the orphans and on Whom the widows depend, is the same God that will protect and be there for you!

PRAY FOR THE ETHNIC GROUP: KANNADA

OCTOBER 29
Jeremiah 50, 51; Psalm 85

Our word for today is **EVERLASTING.**

*They will . . . bind themselves to the LORD in an **everlasting** covenant that will not be forgotten* (Jeremiah 50:5).

It is so comforting to know that the covenant that the Lord makes with us is an everlasting covenant. It is not one that will be forgotten, displaced, put aside or ignored. It doesn't die, and never changes. We can bind ourselves and put our trust in His promises and His covenant with us. He is faithful to His Word, and to all who trust in Him.

PRAY FOR THE ETHNIC GROUP: KAREN

OCTOBER 30
Jeremiah 52; Lamentations 1; Psalm 86

Our word for today is **ABOUNDING IN LOVE**.

*You, LORD, are forgiving and good, **abounding in love** to all who call to you* (Psalm 86:5).

God is a God of providence. Whenever His children call upon His name, He will move heaven and earth to protect them because His love abounds! The greatest love you will ever know is the love of the Father for His children.

PRAY FOR THE ETHNIC GROUP: KASHMIRIS

OCTOBER 31
Lamentations 2, 3, 4; Psalm 87, 88

Our word for today is **NEW**.

*...the LORD's...compassions never fail. They are **new** every morning; great is your faithfulness* (Lamentations 3:22-23).

What do you need today? Maybe you hurt someone and need forgiveness. Possibly you said something stupid (we all do!) and need grace. Or, maybe you had something taken from you, and you need restoration. The wonderful thing about the compassion of the Lord is that it is new and available us every morning. It is out of His compassion for us that He gives exactly what is needed each day. Thank You, Father, for Your faithfulness and that Your compassion is new every morning!

PRAY FOR THE ETHNIC GROUP: KAZAKHS

NOVEMBER 1
Lamentations 5; Ezekiel 1; Psalm 89

Our word for today is **WONDERS.**

*The heavens praise your **wonders**, LORD, your faithfulness too, in the assembly of the holy ones* (Psalm 89:5).

Take a moment to think about how big our God is. When you really stop and think about His wonders and faithfulness to us, it is hard to grasp: Creator of the vast and brilliant universe; the One Who fashioned all the intricacies in the human body—down to the smallest cell; the One Who is always present, all-powerful, mighty, and strong; and the One Who sent from heaven to earth His Only Son as a baby to give us hope, new life, and freedom. Just take a moment and think about how our God, this amazing, wonderful God…loves you!

PRAY FOR THE ETHNIC GROUP: KIKUYU

NOVEMBER 2
Ezekiel 2, 3; Psalm 90

Our word for today is **SPEAK TO YOU.**

*And he said to me, "Son of man, listen carefully and take to heart all the words I **speak to you**"* (Ezekiel 3:10).

You may feel that your prayers are being unanswered, but trust that God is speaking to you. Open yourself up today to intentionally listen to the words God is speaking to you.

PRAY FOR THE ETHNIC GROUP: KONGO

NOVEMBER 3
Ezekiel 4, 5; Psalm 91

Our word for today is **FORTRESS.**

... the LORD "... is my refuge and my fortress, my God, in whom I trust" (Psalm 91:2).

When you were a kid did you ever play with those cardboard boxes that looked like bricks? As a kid, it was fun to imagine building the wall to a castle to keep out the dragons. When you take refuge and trust in the Lord and rest in His stronghold, you are trusting that He will keep and watch over you when the enemy comes to steal, kill and destroy. You remain calm and secure, knowing that you are protected. He is your refuge and fortress, and the One you can trust!

PRAY FOR THE ETHNIC GROUP: KONKANI

NOVEMBER 4
Ezekiel 6, 7; Psalm 92

Our word for today is **FLOURISH.**

The righteous will flourish ... in the courts of our God (Psalm 92:12-13).

Our God is about life, and gives us all that we need to flourish and grow in His Word and through His Spirit. Spend time today reading His Word and allow the Spirit to water and feed your soul. Commit to do this every day, and you will see the fruit of His presence in your life.

PRAY FOR THE ETHNIC GROUP: KOREANS

NOVEMBER 5
Ezekiel 8, 9; Psalm 93

Our word for today is **ETERNITY.**

The LORD reigns... robed in majesty... from all eternity (Psalm 93:1-2).

The Bible warns us about the folly of trusting in temporal riches rather than in the eternal riches promised to God's people. When we put our faith and hope in Him, we partake in the promises of eternity.

PRAY FOR THE ETHNIC GROUP: KURDS

NOVEMBER 6
Ezekiel 10, 11; Psalm 94

Our word for today is **GLORY OF THE LORD.**

... the court was full of the radiance of the glory of the LORD (Ezekiel 10:4).

Another verse that speaks about radiance is Daniel 12:3. Here it says that "... those that lead the many to righteousness [will shine] like the stars in heaven forever and ever." We shine with the radiance of the glory of the Lord as we abide in His presence, and follow in His footsteps.

PRAY FOR THE ETHNIC GROUP: KYRGYZ

NOVEMBER 7
Ezekiel 12, 13, 14; Psalm 95, 96

Our word for today is **SAVE**.

*"... I will **save** my people from your hands. And then you will know that I am the LORD"* (Ezekiel 13:23).

An ever-present help in time of need (see Psalm 46:1), God's desire is to save you from the hand of your enemy. His salvation is not only to remind you of His love for you, but also to remind your enemies that you belong to Him. You are under His protection and care! And, if God be for you, who can stand against you (see Romans 8:31)?

PRAY FOR THE ETHNIC GROUP: LANGO

NOVEMBER 8
Ezekiel 15, 16; Psalm 97

Our word for today is **PROCLAIM**.

*The heavens **proclaim** his righteousness, and all peoples see his glory* (Psalm 97:6).

If you have ever looked through a telescope to view the stars, then you know that though we might see them with our naked eye as white, they are varied colors. Yet, they are all brilliant. Even in space, far away, His order and righteousness are displayed. As you look at the stars tonight, thank Him for His glory and that it can be seen in all things He has created.

PRAY FOR THE ETHNIC GROUP: LATVIANS

NOVEMBER 9
Ezekiel 17, 18; Psalm 98

Our word for today is **RIGHTEOUSNESS.**

> *... The **righteousness** of the righteous will be credited to them...* (Ezekiel 18:20).

The very fact that Jesus died to make each of us righteous should indicate how important righteousness is to God, and what a priceless gift it is. He wants us to be like Him in all ways and made that possible through the Cross: See 2 Corinthians 5:21. What an amazing proclamation. Say it with me now ... I am the righteousness of God in Christ!

PRAY FOR THE ETHNIC GROUP: LITHUANIANS

NOVEMBER 10
Ezekiel 19, 20; Psalm 99

Our word for today is **EXALT.**

> ***Exalt** the LORD our God and worship at his holy mountain, for the LORD our God is holy* (Psalm 99:9).

Today, take a moment to exalt the Lord for His holiness. He is holy and righteous, and commands that we be the same. Thank Jesus for all that was done on the Cross for you, to make you more and more into the image of the Father.

PRAY FOR THE ETHNIC GROUP: LAZ

NOVEMBER 11
Ezekiel 21, 22; Psalm 100

Our word for today is **IN THE GAP.**

*"I looked for someone among them who would build up the wall and stand before me **in the gap**..."* (Ezekiel 22:30).

Jesus Christ stands in the gap for you. He stands between you and a righteous, holy God. He has taken your punishment for sin and your guilt and shame. The Word tells us that sin no longer has a hold on us (see Romans 6:14), and that we have been freed from all condemnation (see Romans 8:1). Thank Him today for standing in the gap for you!

PRAY FOR THE ETHNIC GROUP: LUBA

NOVEMBER 12
Ezekiel 23, 24; Psalm 101

Our word for today is **DWELL WITH ME.**

*My eyes will be on the faithful in the land, that they may **dwell with me**...* (Psalm 101:6).

Dwelling with God, spending time with Him in His presence, is a blessed and precious experience. One day we will enter His "house," never to leave! We will be blessed with the opportunity of dwelling with the Father forever.

PRAY FOR THE ETHNIC GROUP: LUO

NOVEMBER 13
Ezekiel 25, 26; Psalm 102

Our word for today is **RENOWN.**

> But you, LORD, sit enthroned forever; your **renown** endures through all generations (Psalm 102:12).

Think of a famous person on earth; whether their fame was the result of good or bad actions, it was not eternal. But, God has been known from the beginning and will be known throughout all of time. His renown is eternal.

PRAY FOR THE ETHNIC GROUP: MACEDONIANS

NOVEMBER 14
Ezekiel 27, 28, 29; Psalm 103, 104

Our word for today is **SAFETY.**

> "... the people of Israel... will live there in **safety** and will build houses and plant vineyards..." (Ezekiel 28:25-26).

Do you feel safe? I am not talking about the habitat that you dwell in, or the country where you might live. It is possible to feel safe, though everything around you is in chaos. When you trust in the Lord and confess His Word as your protection, you know that no matter where you are... He will keep you safe.

PRAY FOR THE ETHNIC GROUP: MALAYS

NOVEMBER 15
Ezekiel 30, 31; Psalm 105

Our word for today is **HEIR**.

*He gave them the lands of the nations, and they fell **heir** to what others had toiled for* (Psalm 105:44).

You are an heir of God's kingdom! You have rights to eternal life, victory over sin and Satan, the right to use Jesus' name in prayer, the right to the indwelling Holy Spirit, and many more benefits!

PRAY FOR: MOZAMBIQUE

NOVEMBER 16
Ezekiel 32, 33; Psalm 106

Our word for today is **SHOW FAVOR**.

*Remember me, LORD, when you **show favor** to your people…* (Psalm 106:4).

You have God's favor today, and every day! Being the loving Father that He is, He shows favor to us in all things.

PRAY FOR THE ETHNIC GROUP: MALAYALI

NOVEMBER 17
Ezekiel 34, 35; Psalm 107

Our word for today is **RESCUE.**

...so will I look after my sheep. I will rescue them... (Ezekiel 34:12).

When I think of sheep, I think of these little creatures made of stumpy balls of cotton-like fur with black noses that walk around, mouth open wide, "baaa'ing" all the time. That's us! And, what a comfort to know that our Heavenly Shepherd will come searching for us if we get lost, will rescue us if we get stuck in a thicket, and will protect us from the wolves of the world.

PRAY FOR THE ETHNIC GROUP: MALTESE

NOVEMBER 18
Ezekiel 36, 37; Psalm 108

Our word for today is **MY SPIRIT.**

*"I will put **my Spirit** in you and you will live, and I will settle you in your own land..."* (Ezekiel 37:14).

The Word tells us that our bodies are the temples of the Holy Spirit. The Holy Spirit resides in us. He is that still small voice that reminds us of what Christ did, and that we are righteous. He is the One that leads us into a life of godliness. What a precious gift that God has given us—His Spirit!

PRAY FOR THE ETHNIC GROUP: MANCHU

NOVEMBER 19
Ezekiel 38, 39; Psalm 109

Our word for today is **NEEDY.**

*For he stands at the right hand of the **needy**, to save their lives from those who would condemn them* (Psalm 109:31).

As humans, we are all needy. Our flesh fails us, and we need physical sustenance as well as spiritual nourishment. The good news is that we have the Father always with us, who saves us and meets every need.

PRAY FOR THE ETHNIC GROUP: MANDINKA

NOVEMBER 20
Ezekiel 40, 41, 42; Psalm 110

Our word for today is **HEAR.**

*"... look with your eyes, and **hear** with your ears, and set your heart upon all that I shall show you..."* (Ezekiel 40:4, ESV).

The Lord is always speaking. Take a moment to be still and quiet the distractions and pressing thoughts going through your mind, close your eyes (not if you are driving!) and listen. You will see and hear all that He wants you to know.

PRAY FOR THE ETHNIC GROUP: MARATHI

NOVEMBER 21
Ezekiel 43, 44, 45; Psalm 111, 112

Our word for today is **GLORY**.

*... I looked, and behold, the **glory** of the LORD filled the temple of the LORD. And I fell on my face* (Ezekiel 44:4, ESV).

The fear of the Lord is the beginning of wisdom. Exercise wisdom and honor the Lord today through your words, thoughts and actions, and the glory of the Lord will be seen by others through you.

PRAY FOR THE ETHNIC GROUP: MAURITIANS

NOVEMBER 22
Ezekiel 46, 47; Psalm 113

Our word for today is **RAISES THE POOR**.

*He **raises the poor** from the dust and lifts the needy from the ash heap* (Psalm 113:7, ESV).

Jesus was never afraid to touch the poor or sick. In one story He touched a man with leprosy, whose skin was falling off, who probably smelled awful, and who was rejected and separated from society. Jesus touched this poor man, raised him up, and healed him. There is no one too poor, too needy, or too sick for Jesus to touch. He loves the unlovable, the infected, the scorned, and the rejected.

PRAY FOR THE ETHNIC GROUP: MOLDOVANS

NOVEMBER 23
Ezekiel 48; Daniel 1; Psalm 114

Our word for today is **SANCTUARY.**

*Fruit trees... will grow... they will bear fruit, because the water from the **sanctuary** flows to them...* (Ezekiel 47:12).

You know a good tree by its fruit. The ultimate good of a tree is not just to give shade, but to bear fruit. And a good tree bears fruit because of the sanctuary, the water of life that flows to it.

PRAY FOR THE ETHNIC GROUP: MONGO

NOVEMBER 24
Daniel 2, 3; Psalm 115

Our word for today is **LEARNING.**

*To these four young men God gave knowledge and understanding... and **learning**...* (Daniel 1:17).

Do you like learning new things? I know that my daughter, Sarah, loves to learn new languages. I bet if I dropped her in a country with a language that she didn't know, she would be speaking that new language in no time at all. We, as believers, speak a new language every day. We speak the life-giving language of the Spirit and of love, faith and hope. To unbelievers our language may seem foreign. But, to the Lord, it is familiar and sweet to His ears.

PRAY FOR THE ETHNIC GROUP: MONGOLS

NOVEMBER 25
Daniel 4, 5; Psalm 116

Our word for today is **DOMINION.**

*...I praised the Most High...His dominion is an eternal **dominion**...* (Daniel 4:34).

Praise the Lord that His dominion is eternal. We can count on His authority and sovereignty. We can rest and feel secure in His judgments. We know that we are safe under His covering and counsel.

PRAY FOR THE ETHNIC GROUP: NAGA

NOVEMBER 26
Daniel 6, 7; Psalm 117

Our word for today is **PRAISE THE LORD.**

...the faithfulness of the LORD endures forever. **Praise the LORD** (Psalm 117:2).

We have abundant reason to praise God. Our God is full of love, grace, mercy and faithfulness. He never changes—these traits endure forever. He will remain faithful to the end of time. Praise God!

PRAY FOR THE ETHNIC GROUP: NEPALI

NOVEMBER 27
Daniel 8, 9; Psalm 118

Our word for today is **TRIUMPH.**

The LORD is with me; he is my helper. I look in triumph on my enemies (Psalm 118:7).

God can bring even the most extreme defeats into situations of triumph. We see story after story throughout Scripture that illustrates God's help to people in the midst of overwhelming odds.

PRAY FOR THE ETHNIC GROUP: NORWEGIANS

NOVEMBER 28
Daniel 10, 11, 12; Psalm 119:1-55

Our word for today is **ANSWER.**

"... You had no sooner started your prayer when the answer was given..." (Daniel 9:22-23, MSG).

God's unchanging Word has an answer for every problem and circumstance. The Word never fails anyone who stands firm on God's promises.

PRAY FOR THE ETHNIC GROUP: NUBIANS

NOVEMBER 29
Hosea 1, 2; Psalm 119:56-75

Our word for today is **WISE.**

*Those who are **wise** will shine like the brightness of the heavens...* (Daniel 12:3).

You have the mind of Christ as a born-again believer. Speak this in your life and claim it. Jesus had a mind with perfect recall, full of God's wisdom. You, too, have this wisdom which causes you to shine!

PRAY FOR THE ETHNIC GROUP: NUER

NOVEMBER 30
Hosea 3, 4; Psalm 119:76-90

Our word for today is **MY HOPE.**

*My soul faints with longing for your salvation, but I have put **my hope** in your word* (Psalm 119:81).

You can put your hope in God's Word and know, without a doubt, that His Word will come to pass. He never allows His Word to return to Him void (see Isaiah 55:11).

PRAY FOR THE ETHNIC GROUP: ODIA

DECEMBER 1
Hosea 5; Psalm 119:91-112

Our word for today is **JOY OF MY HEART.**

*Your statutes are my heritage forever; they are the **joy of my heart*** (Psalm 119:111).

The life-giving Word of God will bring joy to your heart. It's the kind of joy from the Lord that will strengthen you and keep you in peace, no matter the circumstances that you may be facing. Spend time in the Word today and let the Lord fill you with His joy.

PRAY FOR THE ETHNIC GROUP: OROMO

DECEMBER 2
Hosea 6, 7; Psalm 119:113-136

Our word for today is **ACKNOWLEDGE.**

*"Let us **acknowledge** the L*ORD*... he will come to us like the winter rains, like the spring rains that water the earth"* (Hosea 6:3).

Father, we acknowledge and thank You that You give the cleansing, refreshing rain of Your Spirit when our soul feels dry and thirsty. You are the only One Who can quench our thirst.

PRAY FOR THE ETHNIC GROUP: PARSI

DECEMBER 3
Hosea 8, 9; Psalm 119:137-160

Our word for today is **UNDERSTANDING.**

Your statutes are always righteous; give me **understanding** *that I may live* (Psalm 119:144).

The Word says that the "righteous understand all things" (see Proverbs 28:5). Through Him, we have the understanding that we need to make wise decisions. By knowing Him and through His divine power we have all that we need to live a life of godliness (see 2 Peter 1:3).

PRAY FOR THE ETHNIC GROUP: PASHTUNS

DECEMBER 4
Hosea 10, 11; Psalm 119:161-176

Our word for today is **UNFAILING LOVE.**

"Sow righteousness for yourselves, reap the fruit of **unfailing love** *..."* (Hosea 10:12).

It pays to serve the Lord and build for a harvest. If you sow to the flesh, you are going to reap death, but if you sow to the Spirit, you will reap life and unfailing love!

PRAY FOR THE ETHNIC GROUP: PERSIANS

DECEMBER 5
Hosea 12, 13, 14; Psalm 120, 121

Our word for today is **HELP**.

*My **help** comes from the LORD, the Maker of heaven and earth* (Psalm 121:2).

Never forget, our need for Jesus does not indicate we are flawed. Rather, we would be defective if we refused to recognize the truth of our need for Jesus! He is our Help!

PRAY FOR THE ETHNIC GROUP: POLES

DECEMBER 6
Joel 1, 2; Psalm 122

Our word for today is **NAME OF THE LORD**.

*And everyone who calls on the **name of the LORD** will be saved... there will be deliverance...* (Joel 2:32).

By calling on God in the name of Jesus, and by standing on His Word, you become a person of destiny who opens the door for the mighty power of God to enter every situation. The name of the Lord is powerful!

PRAY FOR THE ETHNIC GROUP: PORTUGUESE

DECEMBER 7
Joel 3; Amos 1; Psalm 123

Our word for today is **ENTHRONED.**

I lift up my eyes to you, to you who sit enthroned in heaven (Psalm 123:1).

The next time that you face a problem that you think is too big for you to handle, think about how big the One Who sits enthroned in heaven is. He can handle it! Go to God and tell Him your need. Believe in His promise that nothing is impossible for Him (see Luke 1:37).

PRAY FOR THE ETHNIC GROUP: PUNJABI

DECEMBER 8
Amos 2, 3; Psalm 124

Our word for today is **HIS PLAN.**

Surely the Sovereign LORD does nothing without revealing his plan to his servants the prophets (Amos 3:7).

God has a vision for everyone. No one is born into this life that God doesn't have a plan and a destiny for. He says His light shines on everyone who comes into this world, so getting a hold of that vision is so key for us.

PRAY FOR THE ETHNIC GROUP: PEDI

DECEMBER 9
Amos 4, 5; Psalm 125

Our word for today is **SURROUND.**

*As the mountains **surround** Jerusalem, so the LORD surrounds his people both now and forevermore* (Psalm 125:2).

There is never a situation in life that He is not there, holding you, and surrounding you with His presence. Sometimes when we are mistreated or abused, we ask God "where were you?" He was there. And, He wants to heal you of the wound that was created by that person's actions or words. Take a moment to hand that wound over to Him, and thank Him for always being with you, and never leaving you to face this world alone.

PRAY FOR THE ETHNIC GROUP: ROHINGYAS

DECEMBER 10
Amos 6, 7; Psalm 126

Our word for today is **WITH JOY.**

*The LORD has done great things for us, and we are filled **with joy*** (Psalm 126:3).

Feeling weak? Want to be strong? Remember the great things that God has done for you and you will walk through life with joy. Remember, it is His joy that is our strength! (See Nehemiah 8:10 and Psalm 28:7.)

PRAY FOR THE ETHNIC GROUP: ROMANIANS

DECEMBER 11
Amos 8, 9; Psalm 127

Our word for today is **FRUIT**.

...I will bring my people Israel back from exile. "... they will make gardens and eat their fruit" (Amos 9:14).

When the Lord restores, He doesn't just make things the way they were, He makes them better. For the people of Israel, He didn't just bring them back to their homeland, He brought them to a land filled with abundant prosperity and provision; gardens and fruit. What do you need restored in your life? Believe that He will not only restore what was lost, but give much more.

PRAY FOR THE ETHNIC GROUP: ROMANI AND ZULU

DECEMBER 12
Obadiah; Jonah 1, 2; Psalm 128, 129

Our word for today is **DELIVERANCE**.

*But on Mount Zion will be **deliverance**; it will be holy, and Jacob will possess his inheritance* (Obadiah 1:17).

God promises deliverance. I'm sure you have experienced moments of deliverance in your life—whether God delivered you from an impossible situation or an unpleasant attitude. He is a great God, and we can count on His promises of deliverance.

PRAY FOR THE ETHNIC GROUP: RUSSIANS AND ZHUANG

DECEMBER 13
Jonah 3, 4; Psalm 130

Our word for today is **MY HOPE.**

I wait for the LORD, my whole being waits, and in his word I put my hope (Psalm 130:5).

We put not only our hope, but also our faith in the Lord and His Word. God calls faith the "substance of things hoped for" (see Hebrews 11:1). Hope sets a goal, but faith provides the substance for meeting the goal. Put your hope in the Lord, but don't forget to have faith that He will see it through.

PRAY FOR THE ETHNIC GROUP: SARA AND YORUBA

DECEMBER 14
Micah 1, 2; Psalm 131

Our word for today is **PROUD.**

My heart is not proud, LORD, my eyes are not haughty... (Psalm 131:1).

When we exercise pride, our focus is on self, and not Him. Pride is an incorrect belief that God is not enough. Honestly search your heart today. Is there any area where you have exhibited pride? Go to His Word, be filled with His love and receive forgiveness. He is more than enough for any need you have.

PRAY FOR THE ETHNIC GROUP: SARDINIANS AND YAKUTS

DECEMBER 15
Micah 3, 4; Psalm 132

Our word for today is **FILLED WITH POWER.**

*...I am **filled with power**, with the Spirit of the LORD, and with justice and might...* (Micah 3:8).

In 2017 women in Saudi Arabia were given, for the first time, the right to drive an automobile. Once powerless and dependent on others, now they can drive about the country without a male guardian. Through Christ, you can be filled with power daily. Praise God that through the Spirit of the Lord we can move about this earth freely, filled with power, justice and might.

PRAY FOR THE ETHNIC GROUP: SCANDINAVIANS AND XHOSA

DECEMBER 16
Micah 5, 6; Psalm 133

Our word for today is **MERCY.**

*...what does the LORD require of you? To act justly and to love **mercy** and to walk humbly with your God* (Micah 6:8).

Faith is acting uncompromisingly on God's Word. Hearing and acting on God's Word will increase your faith. Increased faith will give you increased power to act according to His will.

PRAY FOR THE ETHNIC GROUP: SCOTTISH AND WELSH

DECEMBER 17
Micah 7; Nahum 1; Psalm 134

Our word for today is **MAKER OF HEAVEN.**

May the LORD bless you from Zion, he who is the
Maker of heaven and earth (Psalm 134:3).

Hallelujah! The Maker of heaven and earth is the One Who walks with you daily. How blessed we truly are to know that nothing is too big and nothing is too small for Him. The God Who created the smallest microbes and the largest stars considers you to be His most valuable creation!

PRAY FOR THE ETHNIC GROUP:
SERBS AND VIETNAMESE

DECEMBER 18
Nahum 2, 3; Psalm 135

Our word for today is **PLEASANT.**

Praise the LORD, for the LORD is good; sing praise to
his name, for that is pleasant (Psalm 135:3).

What satisfaction, and how pleasant it is to know His presence. Like a song that you can't (and never want) to get out your head, the Lord surrounds you with songs of deliverance (see Psalm 32:7). Why not sing along?

PRAY FOR THE ETHNIC GROUP:
SEYCHELLOIS AND UZBEK

DECEMBER 19
Habakkuk 1, 2, 3; Psalm 136, 137

Our word for today is **GLORY.**

*For the earth will be filled with the knowledge of the **glory** of the* LORD *as the waters cover the sea* (Habakkuk 2:14).

God is omnipresent. He is present everywhere, close to everything, next to everyone. He fills heaven and earth. We see His heavenly glory here on earth and are blessed with sharing this glory with others.

PRAY FOR THE ETHNIC GROUP: SHONA AND UYGHUR

DECEMBER 20
Zephaniah 1, 2; Psalm 138

Our word for today is **SEEK THE LORD.**

Seek the LORD, *all you humble of the land, you who do what he commands . . .* (Zephaniah 2:3).

Seek the Lord—He wants to be found by you! Cry out to Him, call His name, open the Word of God and ask Him for direction. Like the father who saw his prodigal son coming from afar, the Lord will run toward you as you seek Him.

PRAY FOR THE ETHNIC GROUP: SINDHIS AND UKRAINIANS

DECEMBER 21
Zephaniah 3; Haggai 1; Psalm 139

Our word for today is **CREATED.**

*For you **created** my inmost being; you knit me together in my mother's womb* (Psalm 139:13).

Everything about you, God sees as beautiful and right. Everything! Nothing about how you were created is a mistake. Nothing... not one thing! God made you just the way you are, for His glory! He has a purpose and plan for your life, a future, to do you good—not harm (see Jeremiah 29:11). You are beautiful and wonderful in His sight!

PRAY FOR THE ETHNIC GROUP: SINHALESE AND TURKMENS

DECEMBER 22
Haggai 2; Zechariah 1; Psalm 140

Our word for today is **GOLD.**

*"The silver is mine and the **gold** is mine," declares the LORD Almighty* (Haggai 2:8).

All precious and priceless things come from and belong to God. Silver, gold, platinum... all precious metals, all worthy causes, all noble and righteous deeds. All good things come from Him, and belong to Him. Praise Him for the good things that He has given to you!

PRAY FOR THE ETHNIC GROUP: SLOVAKS AND TURKS

DECEMBER 23
Zechariah 2, 3; Psalm 141

Our word for today is **BE GLAD.**

*"Shout and **be glad**... For I am coming, and I will live among you," declares the* LORD (Zechariah 2:10).

There is reason every day to shout for joy and be glad for a Child was born, a Son was given. His name is Wonderful, Counsellor, the mighty God, the everlasting Father, the Prince of Peace (see Isaiah 9:6). He is Immanuel... God with us! He is here!

PRAY FOR THE ETHNIC GROUP: SOGA AND TUAREGS

DECEMBER 24
Zechariah 4, 5; Psalm 142

Our word for today is **REFUGE.**

... *"You are my **refuge**, my portion in the land of the living"* (Psalm 142:5).

Running to God for shelter in the tough times is easy, and necessary. But, what about those times when things are going well? What joy it must give the Lord when we remember with thankfulness all that He has done, and run to Him in the good times. He is our Refuge (our hiding place) no matter the circumstances in life—good or bad.

PRAY FOR THE ETHNIC GROUP: SOMALIS AND TSWANA

DECEMBER 25
Matthew 1, 2; Luke 2; Psalm 143

Our word for today is **BABY**.

*"... You will find a **baby** wrapped in cloths and lying in a manger"* (Luke 2:12).

The best gift of all was Jesus. As this baby lay in a manger, no one realized Who He was or how radically He would transform the world. May you have special, wonderful times with Jesus during all your Christmas celebrations!

**PRAY FOR THE ETHNIC GROUP:
SONGHAI AND TIBETANS**

DECEMBER 26
Zechariah 6, 7, 8; Psalm 144, 145

Our word for today is **MY ROCK**.

*Praise be to the LORD **my Rock**, who trains my hands for war, my fingers for battle* (Psalm 144:1).

Lift your hands and hold them with palms and fingers touching each other. Ready to pray, your hands are officially armed for battle. Praise the Lord your Rock, Who hears your prayers, knows the spiritual forces that you are fighting, and has already supplied the victory through Christ Jesus our Lord.

**PRAY FOR THE ETHNIC GROUP:
SONINKE AND TARTARS**

DECEMBER 27
Zechariah 9, 10; Psalm 146

Our word for today is **SHOUT.**

Rejoice greatly, Daughter Zion! **Shout,** *Daughter Jerusalem! See, your king comes to you...* (Zechariah 9:9).

You officially have permission from God to raise your voice—shout! Glorify Him with shouts of praise!

PRAY FOR THE ETHNIC GROUP: SOTHO AND TAIS

DECEMBER 28
Zechariah 11, 12; Psalm 147

Our word for today is **MIGHTY.**

Great is our LORD *and* **mighty** *in power; his understanding has no limit* (Psalm 147:5).

We serve a limitless God. He is powerful and mighty, and gives us the ability to supernaturally overcome any limitations we may face. God doesn't want us to be crushed by our circumstances—He wants us to crush them.

PRAY FOR THE ETHNIC GROUP: SPANIARDS AND TELUGU

DECEMBER 29
Zechariah 13, 14; Psalm 148

Our word for today is **KING**.

*The LORD will be **king** over the whole earth. On that day there will be one LORD, and his name the only name* (Zechariah 14:9).

There is no other name but the name of Jesus. There are many on this earth who strive to be famous, but their names have limited authority, and will be forgotten. It is only by the name of Jesus that demons are cast out, the sick are healed, the lost are found, and the blind can see. There is no other name and no other authority but JESUS. His authority is eternal; He is King over all!

**PRAY FOR THE ETHNIC GROUP:
SUNDANESE AND TAMILS**

DECEMBER 30
Malachi 1, 2; Psalm 149

Our word for today is **WITH DANCING**.

*Let them praise his name **with dancing** and make music to him with timbrel and harp* (Psalm 149:3).

When was the last time that you danced before the Lord? Take a moment right now to dance in worship to the Lord. Make music with whatever you have (pots and pans will do). Praise Him, for He is worthy!

PRAY FOR THE ETHNIC GROUP: SUKUMA AND TAJIKS

DECEMBER 31
Malachi 3, 4; Psalm 150

Our word for today is **DELIGHTFUL.**

> *"... all the nations will call you blessed, for yours will be a **delightful** land..."* (Malachi 3:12).

Any place where the presence of the Lord resides, is a delightful place. Acknowledge and recognize that He is with you now. He promises that no matter what, He will always be with you (see Matthew 28:20).

PRAY FOR THE ETHNIC GROUP: SWAZI AND SWEDES

Receive Jesus Christ as Lord and Savior of Your Life.

The Bible says, *"That if thou shalt confess with thy mouth the Lord Jesus and shalt believe in thine heart that God raised him from the dead, thou shalt be saved. For with the heart man believeth unto righteousness; and with the mouth confession is made unto salvation"* (Romans 10:9-10).

To receive Jesus Christ as Lord and Savior of your life sincerely pray this prayer from your heart:

Dear Jesus,
I believe that You died for me and that You rose again on the third day. I confess to You that I am a sinner and that I need Your love and forgiveness. Come into my life, forgive my sins, and give me eternal life. I confess You now as my Lord. Thank You for my salvation!

Signed_____

Date_____

Name_____

Address_____

City_____

State/Province_____

Zip/Postal Code_____

Country_____

Phone (H) (_____)_____

Write or call... We will send you information to help you with your new life in Christ: Marilyn Hickey Ministries • P.O. Box 6598 • Englewood, CO 80155 • For prayer or information on product orders call TOLL-FREE at 888-637-4545. Or visit our website at **www.marilynandsarah.org**.

Prayer Request(s)

Let us join our faith with yours for your prayer needs. Fill out the coupon below and send to

Marilyn Hickey Ministries
P.O. Box 6598
Englewood, CO 80155

Prayer Request(s) _____

_____

_____

_____

Please print.

Name_____

Address_____

City_____

State/Province_____

Zip/Postal Code_____

Country_____

Phone (H) (_____)_____

(W) (_____)_____

If you want prayer immediately, call our Prayer Center at **888-637-4545**. Or visit our website at **www.marilynandsarah.org**.

TOUCHING YOU WITH THE LOVE OF JESUS!

Marilyn Hickey
PRAYER CENTER

When was the last time that you could say, "He touched me, right where I hurt"? No matter how serious the nature of your call, we're here to pray the Word and show you how to touch Jesus for real answers to real problems.

Call us and let's touch Jesus, together!
888-637-4545
WE CARE!